DUKE UNIVERSITY
THE FIRST ONE HUNDRED YEARS

1924

DUKE UNIVERSITY THE FIRST ONE HUNDRED YEARS

2024

WRITTEN *by* CAROLYN GERBER

DESIGNED *by* LACEY CHYLACK

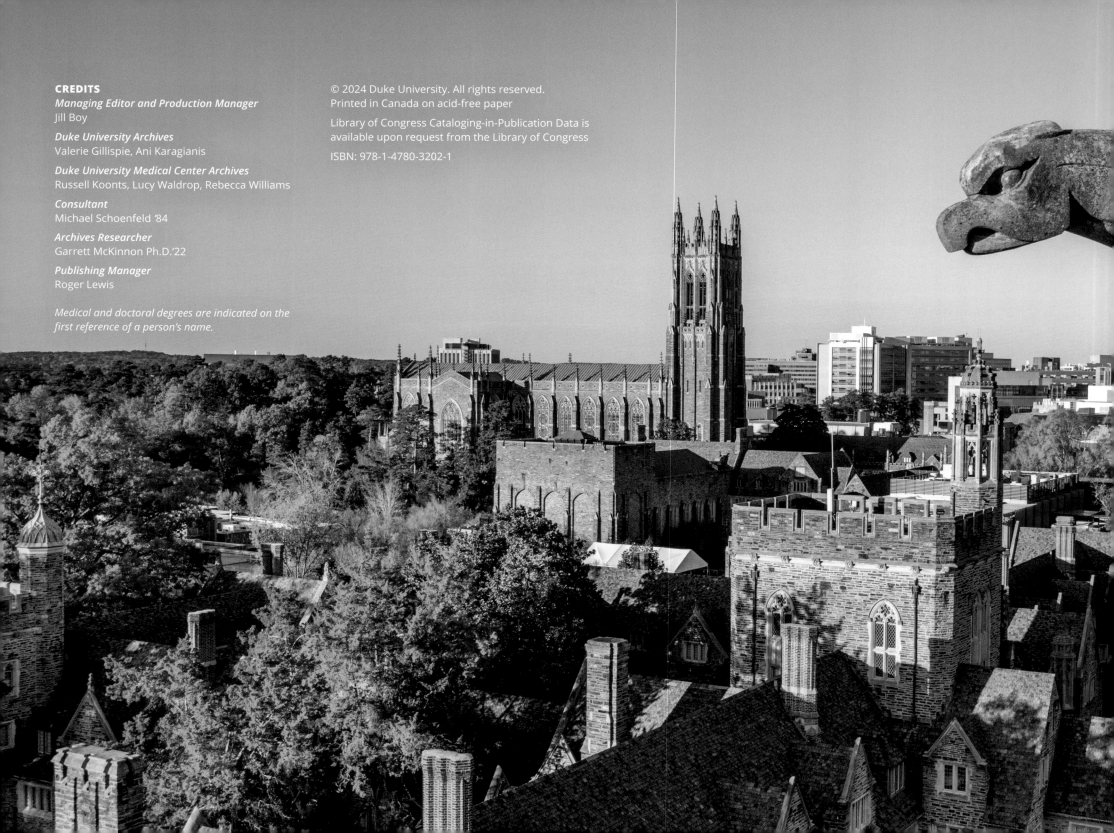

CREDITS

Managing Editor and Production Manager
Jill Boy

Duke University Archives
Valerie Gillispie, Ani Karagianis

Duke University Medical Center Archives
Russell Koonts, Lucy Waldrop, Rebecca Williams

Consultant
Michael Schoenfeld '84

Archives Researcher
Garrett McKinnon Ph.D.'22

Publishing Manager
Roger Lewis

*Medical and doctoral degrees are indicated on the
first reference of a person's name.*

Library of Congress Cataloging-in-Publication Data is
available upon request from the Library of Congress

ISBN: 978-1-4780-3202-1

CONTENTS

◄ *A carved stone eagle on the southwest corner of the Clocktower on* **Crowell Quad** *overlooks Duke University's West Campus.*

LETTER *from the* PRESIDENT

The story of Duke University's first century is one of extraordinary ascent in higher education: the remarkable and somewhat improbable transformation of a small, Southern liberal arts college into an internationally renowned research university and academic medical center.

It is a story of outrageous ambition—as President Terry Sanford put it—of buildings built, minds enriched, discoveries made, programs created, and a reputation grown. It is a story of the slow and belated transition from a closed campus of the few to an open community for all—a transition that is still continuing.

It is also a story, at its core, about people—the people whose vision made Duke possible, and the extraordinary students, faculty, staff, healthcare providers, coaches, and many others who have come here to teach, discover, visit, and work.

And it is about people dedicated to helping others by advancing education, health care, research, athletics, arts, innovation, and service—with one another and with our partners in the Durham community and across the world.

The pages ahead chronicle this story, decade-by-decade, offering a glimpse of the people and moments that have propelled this great university's progress for its first century and readied it for the next 100 years. It is a story of which we can all be very proud.

As we mark Duke's Centennial, I invite you to join us as we candidly reflect on our history, honor the people and the work that brought us to this point, learn from our past, and celebrate our extraordinary achievements.

I hope you will also join us as we sharpen our focus on the work still to come, renew our commitment to meet the needs of a changing world, always striving for growth and progress, and together chart a course toward an even brighter future.

I am tremendously proud to be a Blue Devil and honored to lead the university as we together mark its Centennial. Thank you for supporting the Duke we have always been—and the even more remarkable Duke we are destined to become.

Vince

VINCENT E. PRICE
PRESIDENT

1920s | A DECADE in RETROSPECT

24

December 11, James B. Duke signs the Indenture of Trust

December 29, Trinity College changes its name to Duke University
▸

*Postcards depict the entrance to **Trinity College** in 1911 and the entrance to the newly renamed—but not yet rebuilt—Duke University in 1925.*

25

▸ **Yasuko Ueno** *is the first known Asian woman to graduate from Duke*

Rebuilding *of East Campus begins*

James B. Duke makes an additional bequest to establish the **School of Medicine, School of Nursing,** *and* **Duke University Hospital**

Andres Rodriguez-Diago Y Gomez *is the first known Latin American student to enroll at Duke University*

June 10, First class graduates from **Duke University**

October 25, James B. Duke dies

26

Graduate School of Arts and Sciences *(now The Graduate School) founded*

School of Religion *(now Duke Divinity School) founded*

Trinity College Press, *founded in 1921, becomes* **Duke University Press**

Eddie Cameron *hired at Duke*
▾

In 1926, **Edmund "Eddie" Cameron** *was hired at Duke as the coach for the freshman teams for baseball, basketball, and football. He became the head basketball coach in 1929. His teams won 226 games over 14 seasons.*

27

Wilburt Davison, M.D., *becomes the first dean of the Duke University School of Medicine and Hospital*

Construction of **West Campus** *begins*
▸

Duke awards first Ph.D. degrees to Frederick Holl and Dean Rumbold

January 4, Benjamin Newton Duke, brother of James B. Duke and a trustee of Trinity since 1889, dies

Rose M. Davis becomes the first woman to earn a Ph.D. from Duke

Baseball coach Jack Coombs hired by Duke

October 5, Duke hosts its first game in a new stadium, and the Blue Devil mascot makes its first appearance

Building permit, 1928
This building permit, issued by the City of Durham on January 14, 1928, authorized Duke University to "build a group of buildings" on a "new University Campus." At the time, the cost of $7 million represented the largest building permit ever issued by the City of Durham.

May Day, 1928 *May Day celebrations at Duke date back to 1921, when Duke was Trinity College, and included a spring carnival, performances, and the crowning of the May Queen.*

Stone *was transported from the quarry in Hillsborough by steam engine train. Railroad tracks were laid across West Campus to bring the stone all the way to the construction site.*

19

20s

*The **West Campus cornerstone** was set by **Doris Duke**, daughter of James B. Duke, on June 5, 1928. Originally placed in the West Campus Union, the stone was moved to the Library tower shortly thereafter.*

Duke University was born on December 11, 1924. On that day, **James B. Duke** signed his Indenture of Trust and changed history for Duke, Durham, and the Carolinas. With $40 million, the tobacco entrepreneur created a philanthropic foundation called The Duke Endowment—and designated that $6 million would be given to Trinity College in Durham, which would soon change its name to Duke University to honor his father, **Washington Duke**.

By 1924, Trinity College was a small Southern liberal arts college with a strong academic reputation. Originally founded in 1838 by Methodists and Quakers as a one-room schoolhouse in rural Randolph County, North Carolina, the college fell on hard financial times after the Civil War. In 1887, the college gained an ambitious president in **John Franklin Crowell**, Ph.D., who felt that the college would benefit from being located in an urban environment. At the same time, civic leaders of the rapidly growing tobacco town of Durham believed that a college would add cultural prestige to their "New South" city. With the help of Washington Duke, a tobacco industrialist who contributed funds, and **Julian S. Carr**, who donated land, the college agreed to relocate. Trinity College packed up its library and bell on a boxcar and moved to Durham in 1892. One might say that the college and the town chose each other.

Once established in Durham on what is now East Campus, Trinity College became well known in the South for its high academic standards and its forward-thinking approach to education. At a time when co-education was rare in America, Trinity College women were allowed as day students beginning in 1892, and Washington Duke gave $100,000 to the college in 1896 with the stipulation that "women be admitted on equal footing with men." A women's dormitory was promptly built. Later, in 1903, Trinity College established itself even further for its progressive spirit when historian and 1888 Trinity alumnus **John Spencer Bassett**, Ph.D., published an article praising Black educator Booker T. Washington as one of the greatest men in the South in the past 100 years. A public outcry erupted, and Bassett offered to resign, but the Board of Trustees stood firm on the principle of academic freedom and refused to accept his resignation. The "Bassett Affair" put Trinity College on the map as the institution was recognized for its commitment to defend the scholarly pursuits of its faculty.

In 1910, **William Preston Few**, Ph.D., a former professor of English, became president of Trinity College and began to envision a future for the college that included creating a graduate school and producing scholarship to expand the frontiers of knowledge. President Few knew that his dream of building a research university in North Carolina would need a massive infusion of funds to become a reality. The Duke family of Durham had been strong supporters of Trinity College as trustees and benefactors since the 1880s. Beginning in

Duke University president William Preston Few, speaking about the Duke family at the memorial service for Benjamin N. Duke, January 24, 1929:

"They came up out of the grinding poverty that followed the Civil War. They lived through a period of intense sectionalism and bitterness, but the character of all of them came out untouched by these fires of adversity. They refused to live in a dead past or blindly to conform to the traditions of that past. They were quick to realize that the war was over and that there was a new day in the South. They had the vision to see this new day and the courage to live in the light of it. This often brought them into conflict with local sentiment. But they went on, and they were always patient and tolerant of others. In their business, their friendships, their gifts, they knew no distinctions as to religion, politics, race, or social class. They had many obstacles to overcome, but they succeeded in their great undertakings. They not only called us to better things but they showed us the way."

1921, President Few began to suggest the idea to James B. Duke that a partnership between Few's intellectual vision and Duke's philanthropy could create a new institution that would bring tremendous value to the Carolinas and the nation through its teaching, research, and service.

James B. Duke agreed, and with the signing of the Indenture and his gift to Trinity, the trustees of Trinity College changed its name to Duke University, and President Few began to bring the plans of the Indenture to reality. First, the original East Campus was reconceived in a red brick Georgian style, with many new buildings added. The campus grew dramatically with the purchase of land a mile away, and James B. Duke hired the Philadelphia architectural firm of **Horace Trumbauer** to design what would become the Gothic West Campus. Unknown to many at the time, the chief designer of West Campus as well as the new buildings on East Campus was **Julian Abele**, the first Black graduate of the architecture program at the University of Pennsylvania. To acknowledge Abele's role in creating a campus known for its striking architecture, the entire quad on West Campus was renamed Abele Quad in 2016, with four generations of the Abele family attending the dedication ceremony.

With plans for the physical campus underway, President Few proceeded to lead the administrative expansion of a small college into a large research university. The name of Trinity College was retained as the name of the undergraduate college. The School of Law, which had been one of the original departments of Trinity College, became the Duke University School of Law. In 1926, the university took two more steps to fulfill the vision set out in the Indenture, establishing the School of Religion (now Duke Divinity School) and the Graduate School of Arts and Sciences (now The Graduate School).

As the decade drew to a close, the first West Campus facility opened—not a classroom building or the Chapel, but the football stadium. On October 5, 1929, Duke University hosted its first football game, and the Blue Devil mascot made its first appearance. Duke lost to Pittsburgh, 52 to 7.

In a letter to James B. Duke in 1914 that would prove far-sighted, President Few wrote: "I am particularly anxious that you shall get enduring personal satisfaction and happiness out of what you have done for Trinity College, because you are able to feel that through it you have done some permanent good upon the earth." ∎

A VISION

When James B. Duke created and signed the Indenture of Trust in 1924, he provided for the educational institution that would become known as Duke University, and he set forth his hopes for its leadership in higher education:

"I have selected Duke University as one of the principal objects of this trust because I recognize that education, when conducted along sane and practical, as opposed to dogmatic and theoretical, lines, is, next to religion, the greatest civilizing influence. I request that this institution secure for its officers, trustees, and faculty men of such outstanding character, ability, and vision as will insure its attaining and maintaining a place of real leadership in the educational world, and that great care and discrimination be exercised in admitting as students only those whose previous records show a character, determination, and application evincing a wholesome and real ambition for life." ■

James B. Duke

THE DUKE ENDOWMENT

*With his Indenture of Trust in 1924, James B. Duke created The Duke Endowment. Today, **The Duke Endowment** is one of the largest philanthropic foundations in America. Separate from the Duke University endowment, The Duke Endowment is a private nonprofit headquartered in Charlotte. Over its 100-year history, it has awarded approximately $4.5 billion in grants to organizations in the Carolinas, including nearly $2 billion to Duke University and Duke Health. The Duke Endowment supports specific program areas that were set out in the Indenture: health care, child and family well-being, the rural Methodist church, and four institutions of higher learning in the Carolinas: Duke University, Davidson College, Furman University, and Johnson C. Smith University, a historically Black university in Charlotte.*

VOICES

WILBURT C. DAVISON
and the founding of the
SCHOOL OF MEDICINE

In 1926, President Few recruited Wilburt Cornell Davison from Johns Hopkins University to be the founding dean of the Duke University School of Medicine—a position he held until 1960. A pediatrician by training, Davison also served as chair of pediatrics until 1954.

The son of a Methodist minister, Davison graduated with honors from Princeton University and then studied at Oxford University on a Rhodes Scholarship, where he was one of the last students of the great medical educator Sir William Osler. Davison completed his medical degree at Johns Hopkins and was a rising star in pediatrics there when he accepted the charge at age 35 to build and direct the new Duke University School of Medicine and Hospital. Strongly influenced by his mentor Osler, Davison brought a fresh new approach to health care and medical education and persuaded other brilliant young faculty from Johns Hopkins to join him in the new venture at Duke.

Davison also looked beyond Duke's walls to improve clinical care in North Carolina. Working with leaders of The Duke Endowment, Davison surveyed the healthcare landscape across the state. Informed by what he learned about the challenges of poverty and rural communities, Davison established training programs at Duke for hospital administrators to build capacity in the state.

Under Davison's leadership, within five years Duke was ranked in the top 10 percent of hospitals in the nation. The Davison Building, housing the dean's office of the School of Medicine on West Campus, is named in his honor. ■

OVER THE AIRWAVES

Excerpt of a radio address given by **Wilburt Davison** over Raleigh station WBTW on April 9, 1929, about the establishment of the Duke University School of Medicine and Hospital.

"I wish to express my pleasure for this opportunity to present the plans of the new Hospital and Medical School which are being built in Durham. There are at least six factors which are essential for the success of a medical school—the buildings, the staff, the students, the type of teaching, the service to the community, and last, but not least, the cooperation of the public and of the members of the medical profession in the State. It is the great desire of everyone connected with Duke University to carry out the plans for the first five of these essentials that the sixth one, namely, your cooperation, will be merited, for only by working together can this Hospital and Medical School fill the place which Mr. Duke intended. We all wish you to regard this Hospital and School as yours. Any suggestions which will increase the service of this school to the State will be more than welcomed."

FOUNDATION

*Construction of the **School of Medicine** was begun on September 1, 1927, and was completed in 1930.*

1920s

*A **test stone wall**, built in 1925.*

DUKE STONE

When West Campus was being designed, university leaders wanted the new university to have the collegiate Gothic look of the elite universities in the Northeast. A local quarry near Hillsborough was found to have an interesting stone featuring more than a dozen shades of color, including blue, gray, brown, and orange, formed by ancient volcanic activity. The university purchased the entire quarry and has been using the stone in construction for the past 100 years. The distinctive "Duke stone" has become an iconic and recognizable feature of West Campus.

__A. C. Lee__ (above, left) was the chief engineer of Duke University and the Duke Construction Company from 1926 to 1960. (The university formed its own construction company in 1927 in order to build West Campus.) __Horace Trumbauer__ (above, right) owned the architectural firm that was hired to design both East and West Campuses. The primary designer of West Campus, as well as many of the East Campus buildings, was __Julian F. Abele__ (right), a prominent Black architect and chief designer with the Trumbauer firm.

Duke · University
Durham · North · Carolina.
Horace · Trumbauer · Architect.

This **architectural drawing of West Campus,** *circa 1925, was one of the early designs produced by the Horace Trumbauer firm of Philadelphia. It very closely matches the actual buildings that were built— except for the obelisk in the traffic circle and the lake where the Duke Gardens are now located.*

East Campus Union, *now home of the Marketplace, spring 1927. Pictured is Charles Wesley Clay A.B.'29, B.D.'32, who would go on to become a United Methodist pastor and missionary in Brazil.*

Baldwin Auditorium *construction, mid-1920s.*

TEAMS

Program *for first football game.*
◀

Kickoff *of first game.*
▶

Aerial view *of Duke Stadium on October 5, 1929.*
▼

FOOTBALL

The **first football game** *was played at Duke Stadium on October 5, 1929. The stadium was the first facility to open on West Campus. The Blue Devils played Pittsburgh before 25,000 spectators. (Duke lost, 52 to 7.) The stadium was named for legendary Duke football coach Wallace Wade in 1967.*

1920s

BASEBALL

In the spring of 1929, the Duke baseball team compiled a 13–5 record in its first season under head coach and former major league pitcher **Jack Coombs** (left). Over 24 years as Duke's coach, Coombs would lead his teams to 381 wins—a school record. Duke's baseball field was dedicated in his honor in 1951.

Duke baseball team, **1925–26.**

1920s

Student life, *1920s.*

Hiking Club, *1924, organized in 1923 by women students.*

In October 1926, the Athena and Brooks Literary Societies combined to form the **League of Women Voters**. *This group was active for a number of years in stimulating interest in local (campus) as well as national political issues. It ceased functioning in 1936–37.*

Members of **Delta Phi Rho Alpha**, *an honorary athletic association, 1924.*

The name **"Blue Devils"** *for Duke's sports teams actually started in 1922, when Duke was still Trinity College. The editors of the* Trinity Chronicle *held a referendum on possible names, but there was no clear winner. Instead, the editors chose "Blue Devils," a name that referred to the Chasseurs Alpins, who were elite French soldiers during World War I nicknamed "les Diables Bleus" because of their blue uniforms, capes, and berets. Blue Devils eventually caught on.*

Lapel pin *featuring the phrase "A la gloire des Diables Bleus" (translation: To the glory of the Blue Devils).*

This rolling pin was given to pledges of **Delta Phi Rho Alpha** *during sorority rush.*

1930s | A DECADE *in* RETROSPECT

Commencement, 1931
Graduates process toward Page Auditorium before an unfinished Duke Chapel.

30

▲

Trinity College opens *on West Campus;* **Woman's College opens** *on East Campus*

▸

October 22, **Duke Chapel cornerstone set**

Parapsychology Lab *opens at Duke under the leadership of Joseph Rhine, Ph.D., and Joseph Gaither Pratt, Ph.D.*

July 21, **Duke University Hospital** *opens for patients*

School of Medicine *opens*

31

The School of Nursing *opens, enrolling 24 undergraduates, all women*

32

Duke Chapel, still incomplete, is first used for **commencement**

▸ *The first class of the* **Duke University School of Nursing** *graduates in 1933.*

33 **34** **35** **36** **37** **38** **39**

Handel's Messiah *is performed for the first time in Duke Chapel, starting an annual tradition*

Eleanor Beamer Easley, M.D., *is the first woman to complete the four-year medical school program*

Duke Chapel *is finished and consecrated*

Duke surgeon J. Deryl Hart, M.D., introduces ultraviolet (UV) lamps into operating rooms to reduce infections

Hertha Sponer, *Ph.D., becomes the first woman faculty member hired in the Physics Department*

Mary Duke Biddle Trent Semans, *granddaughter of Benjamin N. Duke and great-granddaughter of Washington Duke, enrolls at Duke University at the age of 15*

Richard Nixon *graduates from Duke Law School*

The brain tumor program is established at Duke—one of the first in the U.S.— and is named the **Preston Robert Tisch Brain Tumor Center** *in 2005*

School of Forestry *opens*

College of Engineering *organized (now the Pratt School of Engineering)*

Duke admitted to the Association of American Universities (AAU)

Duke University Marine Lab *opens*

The Duke football team is undefeated, untied, and unscored upon, earning the nickname "The Iron Dukes"

Dedication of the gardens named in honor of Sarah P. Duke, wife of Benjamin Duke

Duke loses its first Rose Bowl to USC

In 1938–39, Duke celebrates the centennial of its founding as Brown's Schoolhouse in 1838

Duke University **Marine Lab Sign,** *ca. 1938.*

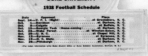

Academic Quad *as seen from the Davison Building, ca. 1931.*

19

30s

Freshmen *arrive by train, 1930s.*

When students arrived on campus in the fall of 1930, they found a transformed Duke University: The newly constructed West Campus opened to students and faculty, and East Campus, the older site of Trinity College, was designated as the Woman's College, with **Alice Mary Baldwin**, Ph.D., as its first dean.

When West Campus was built in the late 1920s and early 1930s— during the Great Depression—it was the largest construction project in the South at the time. The campus had a remarkable architectural unity, rare for American colleges, and was enlivened by striking details of carved stonework, including playful gargoyles. After visiting Duke, the author Aldous Huxley wrote in 1937, "These buildings are genuinely beautiful . . . the most successful essay in neo-Gothic that I know."

In his address to students at the opening of the new school year in 1930, President Few drew on the theme of construction as he urged students "to become builders—builders of colleges, builders of education, builders of causes—and so become useful and happy servants of humanity." In that same builder's spirit, the early 1930s saw the young university take major steps forward in carrying out the vision of James B. Duke to provide teaching and training that would serve society.

Duke University Hospital opened on July 21, 1930, with thousands of curious visitors attending the opening day ceremonies. The hospital boasted 408 beds and teaching facilities such as classrooms and a library. That October, the first students enrolled in the Duke School of Medicine—53 first-year students and 17 third-year students, including four women. The first class had been selected from 3,000 applicants. The hospital had student and staff dormitories, and the medical students studied, ate, and slept there.

The next year, the Duke University School of Nursing and its inaugural dean, **Bessie Baker**, B.S., R.N., welcomed Duke's first 24 nursing students, all women, for the three-year degree program. The *Chronicle* hailed them with words that have proved prescient: "They will prove an asset to the cause of women, and their school will grow to be one of the finest in the university."

In addition to the Schools of Medicine and Nursing, additional academic programs were organized in the 1930s that continue to provide strong intellectual leadership to the university today and research that benefits the state and the nation—the School of Forestry and the College of Engineering.

In the mid-1920s, Duke University began to purchase tracts of land that eventually totaled nearly 5,000 acres. Duke Forest was established in 1931, and **Clarence Korstian**, Ph.D., was named as its first director. Duke Forest became a special asset in 1938 when Duke established the School of Forestry, with its mission to advance graduate forestry

Early **engineering classes.**

education in the southeastern United States, and Korstian became the school's founding dean. Today, Duke's Master of Forestry program continues to train leaders in forest management, conservation, and policy as part of the Nicholas School of the Environment.

Another early component of what would become the Nicholas School of the Environment was the Duke University Marine Laboratory. In the 1930s, Duke scientists led by **Arthur Sperry Pearse**, Ph.D., arranged for Duke to purchase Pivers Island, near the town of Beaufort on the North Carolina coast. The first buildings opened in 1938 for use as a summer training and research facility. Today, the Marine Lab provides year-round opportunities for teaching, research, and training for Duke students and faculty as well as visiting scientists from around the world.

Engineering courses had been offered by Trinity College as early as 1887, and even earlier by its predecessor institution, Normal College. Departments were formed after Trinity became Duke: civil and electrical engineering in 1927 and mechanical engineering in 1931. The College of Engineering was formed in 1939, and **William H. Hall** E'09, A.M.'14 became its first dean, overseeing 201 students. Engineering was originally housed on East Campus. Today, the Pratt School of

Engineering at Duke enrolls more than 1,200 undergraduates across five majors and an interdisciplinary major, as well as nearly 1,000 graduate students in master's and Ph.D. programs.

A sign of the gathering storm clouds in Europe, the federal government sent an urgent request in 1933 to college and university presidents across the United States to ask them to consider hiring scholars who had been victims of political persecution in Germany. The list included "Jewish scholars; scholars with Jewish antecedents or those connected with Jews by marriage; and non-Jewish scholars whose convictions made them unacceptable to the German Government." President William P. Few replied the next day to signal Duke's strong interest. All told, Duke employed six scholars who were fleeing Germany in the 1930s, including **Hertha Sponer**, whose work on molecular spectroscopy had made her one of the two most outstanding women physicists in the world.

While the athletic rivalry between Duke and the University of North Carolina was already fierce by the 1930s, a new partnership was also beginning. President Few developed a good relationship with UNC president Frank Porter Graham, and the two schools shared resources and collaborated in several academic areas. In 1938, President

William Preston Few
*with First Lady of the United
States* **Eleanor Roosevelt**
*on the steps of Duke Chapel,
June 11, 1934.*

Graham nominated Duke
for membership in the
Association of American
Universities, or AAU, and
advocated for its inclusion in
the prestigious organization.
Thanks in part to this support, Duke was approved for membership
in the AAU and took its place among this elite group of research
universities.

As Duke University moved into a new decade, it strove to keep the
traditions of Trinity College alive at the heart of the new university.
Duke adopted Trinity College's motto, *Eruditio et Religio*, or knowledge
and faith. Speaking at Duke's commencement in 1931, President Few
interpreted the meaning of the motto for the mission of the university
to provide knowledge for the world: "Here stand side by side science
and religion, science and scholarship completely given to the full,
untrammeled pursuit of the truth and religion with its burning passion
for righteousness in the world—and commit the University in its very
inception alike to excellence that dwells high among the rocks and to
service that goes out to the lowliest." ∎

Duke University West Campus aerial view, ca. 1930
*This photograph, taken from the south, is the earliest-
known aerial view of West Campus. The newly constructed
buildings opened for students in the fall of 1930. On the left
side of the image is the building site of the Chapel, which
would be dedicated in 1935.*

Members of the first graduating class of the **School of Medicine**. *The Class of 1932 was a two-year class composed of transfer students.*

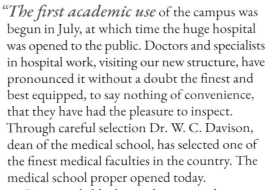

Frances Brooks and Dick Goode, **1939 class presidents,** at commencement.

The surviving members of the **"Old Trinity" faculty** at Duke's combined 1939 commencement and centennial celebration. Left to right: Jerome Dowd, Robert L. Flowers, and Edwin Mims, Ph.D.

VOICES

OPENING THE NEW CAMPUS

Chronicle article, "President Few Speaks at Exercises Formally Opening the New Plant," Wednesday, October 1, 1930

"The first academic use of the campus was begun in July, at which time the huge hospital was opened to the public. Doctors and specialists in hospital work, visiting our new structure, have pronounced it without a doubt the finest and best equipped, to say nothing of convenience, that they have had the pleasure to inspect. Through careful selection Dr. W. C. Davison, dean of the medical school, has selected one of the finest medical faculties in the country. The medical school proper opened today.

It is remarkable that such a tremendous building project should be completed and turned over to the students and faculty in such a short span of time. There has never been a time in the history of any institution when the plant was finished and opened for use as an entire unit until we opened our new twenty-million-dollar home, which consists of 31 buildings. There are, however, two buildings not yet completed—the new chapel and the chemistry building. The chemistry building will be completed in about six or seven months, but the exquisite chapel will require another year's work before it will be complete. Two million dollars is being spent on the structure. It will be, of course, of the same English Gothic architecture as the other buildings, and is likewise being built of native stone from the university's own quarry near Hillsboro [*sic*]. Experts have commented

very highly upon the physical arrangement of Duke's new unit of buildings. Every detail was taken into consideration before plans were drawn up or work begun. The campus is, therefore, very near to ideal. The huge hospital and school of medicine, the law school, the graduate school, the undergraduate school, the school of religion, the administrative offices all have separate edifices. The union, which is the center of all student activity, contains the dining hall and in addition a drug and book store, post office, barber shop, haberdashery, and a separate office for all campus activities.

On the women's campus the six hundred women are housed in handsome brick buildings, made more strikingly beautiful by tall Grecian columns. It contains a complete plant within itself, but bus transportation brings the girls within access of all the academic advantages of the men's unit.

The athletics facilities on the new campus are exceptionally well arranged. Last year our new stadium with a capacity at present of thirty-five thousand was dedicated. A score of new tennis courts have been erected on the new campus, and there are various athletic fields which are being used for different sports. The handsome new gymnasium has also been finished and is being used for the first time this year.

With the formal opening ceremonies in the background now, there is every indication of a most successful year for Duke University." ■

1930s GARDENS

Sarah Pearson Duke, *widow of Benjamin N. Duke, and her daughter,* **Mary Duke Biddle**.

Sarah P. Duke Gardens iris beds, *before 1939.*

DUKE GARDENS

Frederic Hanes, *M.D., arrived at Duke in 1930 as one of the first members of the faculty hired at the School of Medicine. He became chair of the Department of Medicine in 1933 and lived in one of the newly built faculty houses on campus at 614 Chapel Drive. As he walked each day to the hospital, he began to envision a garden devoted to his favorite flower, the iris.*

Hanes proposed the idea to **Sarah P. Duke**, *widow of Benjamin N. Duke, and she donated $20,000 to build a garden. By 1935, 40,000 irises, 25,000 daffodils, and thousands of other flowers had been planted. Unfortunately, the garden was washed out by flooding and never recovered.*

Sarah P. Duke died in 1936, and Hanes turned to her daughter, **Mary Duke Biddle**, *with a proposal to build an entirely new garden—on higher ground this time. This new garden, with its distinctive terraces, was designed by the well-known landscape architect* **Ellen Biddle Shipman** *(the two women were related by marriage). The Sarah P. Duke Gardens were dedicated in April 1939.*

Today, Sarah P. Duke Gardens is one of America's most beautiful gardens, open to the public and welcoming more than 300,000 visitors each year from all over the world. The gardens feature four distinct areas: the original Terraces, the H. L. Blomquist Garden of Native Plants, the W. L. Culberson Asiatic Arboretum, and the Doris Duke Center Gardens, including the Charlotte Brody Discovery Garden. Duke Gardens sponsors education and cultural programs throughout the year and forms an important bridge between Duke and the Durham community.

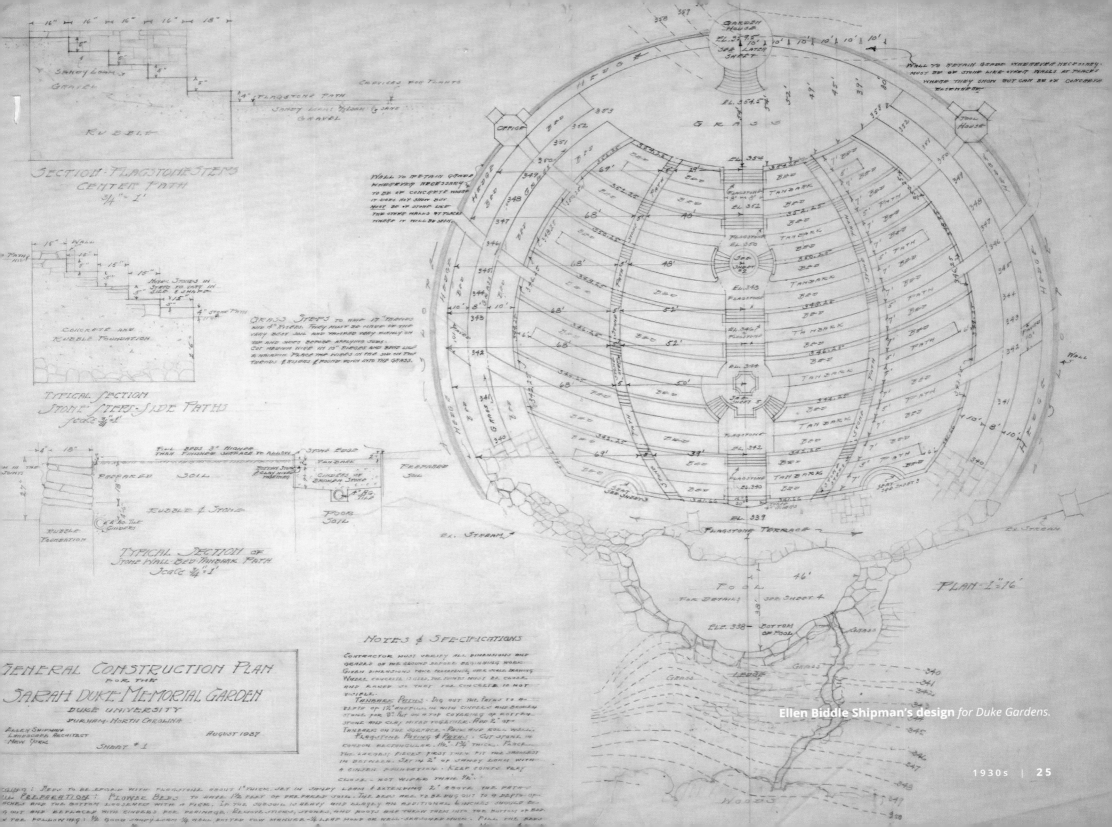

Ellen Biddle Shipman's design *for Duke Gardens.*

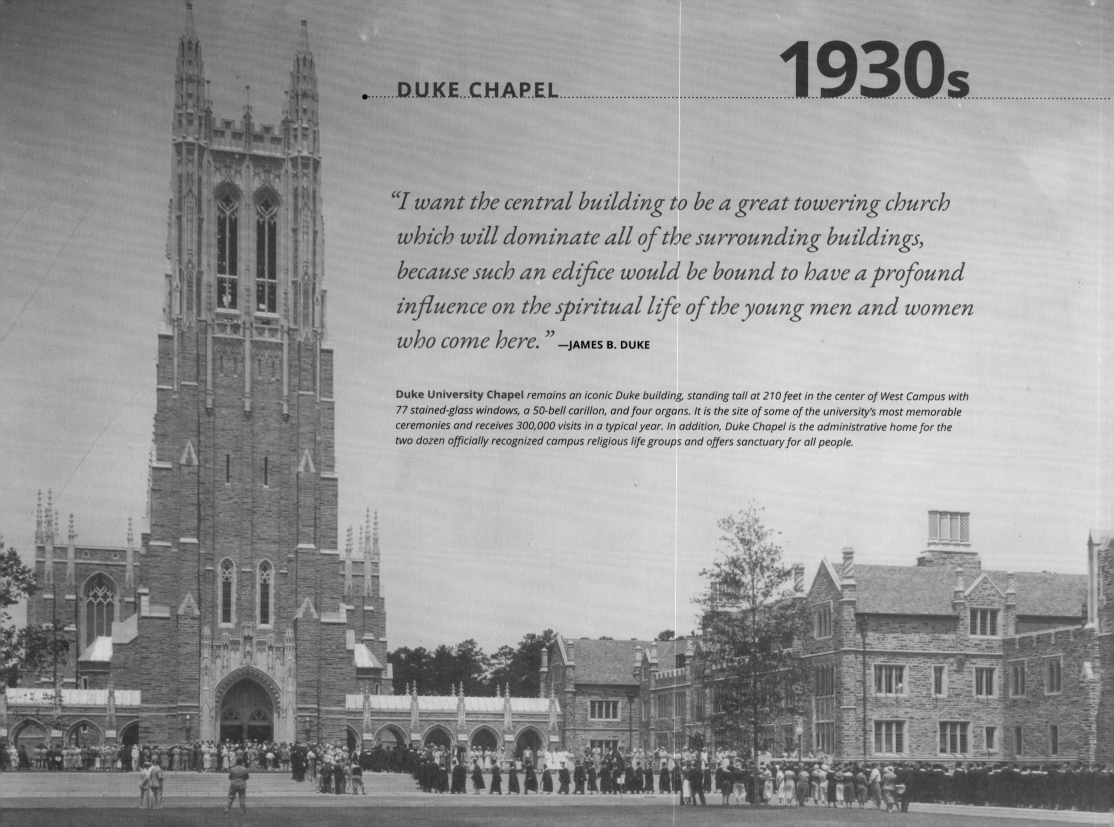

1930s

"I want the central building to be a great towering church which will dominate all of the surrounding buildings, because such an edifice would be bound to have a profound influence on the spiritual life of the young men and women who come here." —JAMES B. DUKE

Duke University Chapel *remains an iconic Duke building, standing tall at 210 feet in the center of West Campus with 77 stained-glass windows, a 50-bell carillon, and four organs. It is the site of some of the university's most memorable ceremonies and receives 300,000 visits in a typical year. In addition, Duke Chapel is the administrative home for the two dozen officially recognized campus religious life groups and offers sanctuary for all people.*

The *The* LARGEST BELL, 1932

*Standing behind the largest bell in the **Duke Chapel carillon** are (from left to right) President William P. Few; Dean W. H. Wannamaker; Professor (and future president) Robert L. Flowers; and F. C. Godfrey, a representative of Taylor Bell Foundry of Loughborough, England.*

*Mary Frances Lehnerts performs during the **Vocarillon concert**, August 17, 1939.*

DUKE FOREST

*In 1938, **Clarence F. Korstian** (above) was named founding dean for the newly created **School of Forestry**. He was instrumental in developing one of the nation's leading forestry programs while also managing and expanding Duke Forest.*

*Today, **Duke Forest** includes more than 7,000 acres across three counties— Durham, Orange, and Alamance. Managed for teaching, research, and recreational purposes, it is Duke's "outdoor classroom and living laboratory." One of the nation's largest private research forests, Duke Forest currently hosts 47 different research projects, some of which have been active for 90 years and contribute to our understanding of climate change.*

1930s

Crash Davis *was made famous as the character played by Kevin Costner in the 1988 movie* Bull Durham. *But 50 years earlier, the real* Lawrence "Crash" Davis *'41 was captain of the Duke baseball team. After graduating from Duke, Davis played three seasons for the Philadelphia Athletics and later played for the Durham Bulls. Years later, the screenwriter Ron Shelton came across his name and was inspired to write the screenplay for the film.*

Baseball team, *1938.*

Dan Hill *'39 and* Eric Tipton *'39 of the Duke Blue Devils with Coach Wallace Wade, Pasadena, 1938.*

FOOTBALL

Hired in 1931, Wallace Wade *(above, center) proved to be a transformative coach for Duke football. Wade came from the University of Alabama, where he led the Crimson Tide to three national championships in seven years. In writing about his hiring in the February 4, 1931, issue, the* Chronicle *described Wade as having "one of the most brilliant coaching records in the history of southern football." During his tenure, the Blue Devils posted a 110–36 record and reached the Rose Bowl in 1939 and 1942.* Wallace Wade Stadium *was named in his honor in 1967.*

MEN'S GOLF

The Duke men's golf team, led by head coach Ellis "Dumpy" Hagler *(right) captured the Southern Conference championship in 1933 to kick off a dominating two-decade run that included 11 more titles.*

BOXING

Ray Matulewicz *'37 (light heavyweight), shown at left with Coach Addison Warren, and* Danny Farrar *'38 (welterweight) won NCAA boxing titles in 1936. (The last NCAA Boxing Championship was held in 1960.)*

Duke swimming team, *1933.*

"*William Preston Few was no fool. He knew that to establish its name and its claim to greatness, Duke needed strengths in addition to its strictly academic strengths, and he saw athletics as a means to build a sense of internal community and to win this school national acclaim.*"

—**President Richard H. Brodhead**, in his annual address to the faculty, March 19, 2015

ORIGINS

George "Jelly" Leftwich Jr., *Duke's first director of instrumental music, poses with the Blue Devil in 1930. Leftwich composed Duke's fight song,* **"The Blue and White."**

MEMORIES

Elizabeth Hatcher Conner '39 *was a photographer for the* **Duke Chanticleer** *and even converted the closet of her dorm room in Bassett into a darkroom. Hatcher took many photos of the Duke campus and her friends on outings with the co-ed Explorers Club. She later donated her negatives and many of her prints to the* **Duke University Archives***.*

Clockwise from left, **Epworth 201,** *Elizabeth Hatcher's dorm room, spring 1935; friends at Myrtle Beach, 1936; Chapel Drive from the top of Duke Chapel, spring 1939, before the construction of the Allen Building and Few Quad.*

1930s

STUDYING *the* PARANORMAL *at* DUKE

*Led by founding director J. B. Rhine, the **Duke Parapsychology Laboratory** opened in 1935, studying supposed psychic and paranormal experiences such as telepathy, extrasensory perception (ESP), hypnosis, and levitation. In the mid-1960s, Duke closed the Parapsychology Lab as the pseudoscience could not be supported by scientific evidence, but its records are still housed in the Duke Libraries. This exchange of letters between J. B. Rhine and a Lutheran pastor in Washington, D.C., concerns a boy who was "disturbed by poltergeist phenomena." This story later became the basis of the 1971 horror film* The Exorcist.

Physical education *for women students, 1938. Requirements for a bachelor's degree included three hours per week of physical exercise.*

Annual Senior Women's Dinner, *ca. 1930s.*

J. B. Rhine *tests a subject using his ESP cards as a lab assistant looks on.*

1940s | A DECADE *in* RETROSPECT

40

President William Preston Few *dies*

Duke Indoor Stadium opens (renamed Cameron Indoor Stadium in 1972)
▼

41

▲
Robert Lee Flowers *becomes president*

42

▲
January 1, Duke plays Oregon State in the Rose Bowl *in Duke Stadium*

Nora Elisa Recio '46 is the first known Latina student at Duke
▼

Architectural rendering of proposed **Indoor Stadium.**

Incoming freshmen *were required to take both a psychological and English placement test during the week of orientation.*

Women play baseball as part of the **Women's Athletic Association,** *1941.*

Left to right: Fran Ellis, Ann Rankin, Mary Ann Duncan, Betty Bayliss, and Julia Pinnix. The five women were contending for the title of **"Beauty Queen"** of Duke's Summer Session in 1946. Mary Ann Duncan (center) was crowned Queen.

43 **44** **47** **48** **49**

Erwin Road dormitory for nurses constructed (later called Hanes House Annex, and today known as the John Hope Franklin Center)

The Duke Medical School basketball team plays the "Secret Game" against the Eagles of North Carolina College for Negroes (later North Carolina Central University)

Bell Research Building opens as Duke's first dedicated research building; it houses Duke's first electron microscope

The Duke University Loyalty Fund is established; today, the Annual Fund is sustained with gifts from more than 51,000 alumni, parents, students, and friends

Author William Styron graduates from Duke

Hudson Hall opens

A. Hollis Edens, Ph.D., becomes president

Paul Gross, Ph.D., becomes vice president of the Educational Division

The **West Campus Dope Shop** in the basement of the Union building was a popular place to buy snacks and sundries.

Robert Frost was the guest of honor at the annual meeting of the Friends of Duke University Libraries, where he read his poetry aloud and commented on the poems for the enthusiastic audience.

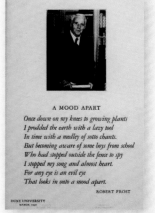

40s

Marine Detachment of the V-12 Unit *on West Campus.*

The 1940s began at Duke with the dedication of Duke Indoor Stadium on January 6, 1940. The plans for the stadium had been drawn up in 1935 by then-basketball coach **Eddie Cameron**, for whom it was later named. Designed by Julian Abele of the Horace Trumbauer firm and constructed at a cost of $400,000, the stadium was the largest indoor arena south of Philadelphia when it opened. From the very beginning, a large number of seats—especially those closest to the floor—were reserved for students.

Sadness struck the university later that year with the sudden death of William Preston Few on October 16. President Few had served as president for 30 years and had presided over the transformation of Trinity College into Duke University. Few oversaw an almost unimaginable expansion of the institution, leading the school's growth from a small college of 363 students and 32 faculty in 1910 to a university that in 1940 boasted 9 schools, 3,716 students, and 476 faculty.

Senior Vice President **Robert Lee Flowers** was named acting president and then president of the university—and was inducted during the 1941 commencement ceremony.

Known fondly on campus as "Professor Bobby Flowers," Duke's new president was held in high esteem and with great affection. An 1891 graduate of the U.S. Naval Academy at Annapolis, Flowers came to North Carolina to teach mathematics and electrical engineering at Trinity College when the college was still located in Randolph County. When the college moved to Durham, Flowers moved with it—one of just four faculty members to do so. As the college grew, Flowers took on administrative roles in addition to his teaching and was considered a natural choice to succeed Few.

While Duke had high hopes for Flowers's presidency, the world had other plans. The American involvement in World War II meant that the university committed itself to one primary focus for the next five years: supporting the national defense effort.

As the draft began and national priorities were clarified, Duke rose to the challenge. The university's missions of teaching, research, and service all pivoted to engage with the war effort, and thousands of Duke students, faculty, employees, and alumni joined the effort.

Duke's research enterprise rapidly focused on topics of military interest. The federal government began to invest strategically in engineering, chemistry, medicine, and other disciplines. Chemistry professor **Paul M. Gross** led a project to devise a bullet that would break up on impact, while other Duke research projects studied the effects of Vitamin B deprivation and ways to control sexually transmitted diseases.

Duke's student ranks grew with an influx of women and soldiers who saw furthering their education as a means to work for the war effort. In 1946, **Marie L. Foote** and **Muriel G. Theodorsen**

Scrap rallies and war bond campaigns *also bridged the gap between the town and campus as everyone pitched in to help the United States support its armed forces.*

Cadet nurses *at Duke.*

became the first two women to graduate from Duke with engineering degrees. After graduation, Theodorsen later reflected that "women in engineering are not undesirable, inept intruders in a traditionally all-male field; but, rather, that we are able co-workers who can carry our own weight and sometimes even excel in this field of untold importance to humanity." Economics, the School of Medicine, and the Divinity School also saw their enrollment of women students increase.

The School of Nursing focused on training nurses for service. The Erwin Road dormitory for nurses was constructed in 1943, with Duke and the Federal Works Administration each contributing $63,650 toward the cost.

Many students gained military training by joining divisions on campus. During the war, Duke activated a Naval Reserve Officers Training Corps (NROTC) and hosted an Army Finance School. Duke was also one of more than 130 colleges and universities nationwide to set up a Navy V-12 program to train and commission officers. Duke offered an accelerated trimester system for the V-12 program and held 10 graduations between 1943 and 1945. Over 4,000 student soldiers came through these programs, including the author William Styron, who transferred to Duke's V-12 program in 1943 and returned after the war to complete his degree in English.

Duke also fostered a culture of patriotic volunteerism among its students and employees, especially through the women-led College Organization for General Service (COGS) and the Duke Civilian

Public Service Unit. These organizations and others brought national attention to Duke.

Duke even staffed an entire U.S. Army hospital, the 65th General Hospital Unit, with Duke students, alumni, and faculty. Members of the unit trained on West Campus before leaving for England, where the 65th carried out lifesaving care for over 17,000 soldiers in Europe during the war, earning many distinguished citations.

In the Law School, many faculty members left for wartime service, and student enrollment dropped precipitously. For several years, the law school of Wake Forest College relocated to Duke because of low enrollment. After the war, returning veterans enrolled in numbers that grew the student population to an unprecedented size for the next five years.

As the war and the subsequent pressure of the transition to a peacetime economy hung over the university, early in 1948 President Flowers announced his retirement and was named to the newly created post of chancellor. When he died in 1951, he had served Trinity College and Duke University for more than 60 years.

On October 22, 1949, Duke University held its first presidential inauguration ceremony—although **A. Hollis Edens** was actually the university's third president. Held on the quad in front of Duke Chapel, with delegates from academic institutions around the world attending, the ceremony became the model for future inaugurations of Duke presidents. ■

Raphael Lemkin *(above), a lawyer and scholar of human rights who coined the term "genocide," spent the 1941–42 academic year as a visiting lecturer at Duke University School of Law. Born in Russia to a Polish Jewish family, Lemkin became a leader and advocate for the creation of international criminal law for the protection of human rights. During World War II, Lemkin came to the United States as a refugee and was invited to teach at Duke by Duke Law professor* **Malcom McDermott** *(right) with whom Lemkin had previously collaborated on academic projects. Later, Lemkin served in the U.S. government as a special adviser on foreign affairs to the War Department. The passage of the Genocide Convention at the United Nations in 1948 is attributable in part to his tireless work.*

Carvings of a **judge's wig***, the scales of justice, and a book adorn the main entrance of the original Duke School of Law Building on West Campus—today known as the Languages Building. In 1962, the* **School of Law** *moved to its new building off Science Drive.*

The **Lemkin Rule of Law Guardian** *medal, awarded by the Bolch Judicial Institute at Duke University School of Law, is named in his honor.*

1940s

65TH GENERAL HOSPITAL

The idea of a **Duke hospital army unit** was proposed by Wilburt C. Davison, then dean of the School of Medicine. Activated in July 1942, the army reserve unit was staffed entirely by Duke medical faculty, alumni, and current or former house staff. From 1944 to 1945, the 65th General Hospital was set up at Redgrave Park in Suffolk, England. The unit cared for wounded soldiers who had been evacuated from front-line hospitals in Europe, treating over 17,250 patients with a very low mortality rate of 0.4 percent.

Nurses and servicemen of the **65th General Hospital** waiting to be shipped overseas. After 15 months of training at Fort Bragg, the unit left for England in 1943.

President Ronald Reagan's 1982 letter to the members of the 65th on the fortieth anniversary, congratulating them on their "outstanding record overseas."

A sculpture was dedicated in 2002 near Duke Clinic in Durham "to honor the 65th, and all other men and women of **Duke University Medical Center** who have served our country in the armed forces."

THE WHITE HOUSE
WASHINGTON

April 14, 1982

I am delighted to extend my warm greetings to all those gathered to commemorate the 40th anniversary of the call to active duty of the 65th General Hospital Unit.

The 65th was sponsored and staffed by the faculty and graduates of Duke University Medical School to care for the casualties of the Eighth and Ninth Air Forces in World War II. Your Unit compiled an outstanding record overseas and deserves the respect and gratitude of all Americans for the devoted service you performed for our fighting forces.

Congratulations on reaching this significant milestone. I wish you good luck in the future.

Ronald Reagan

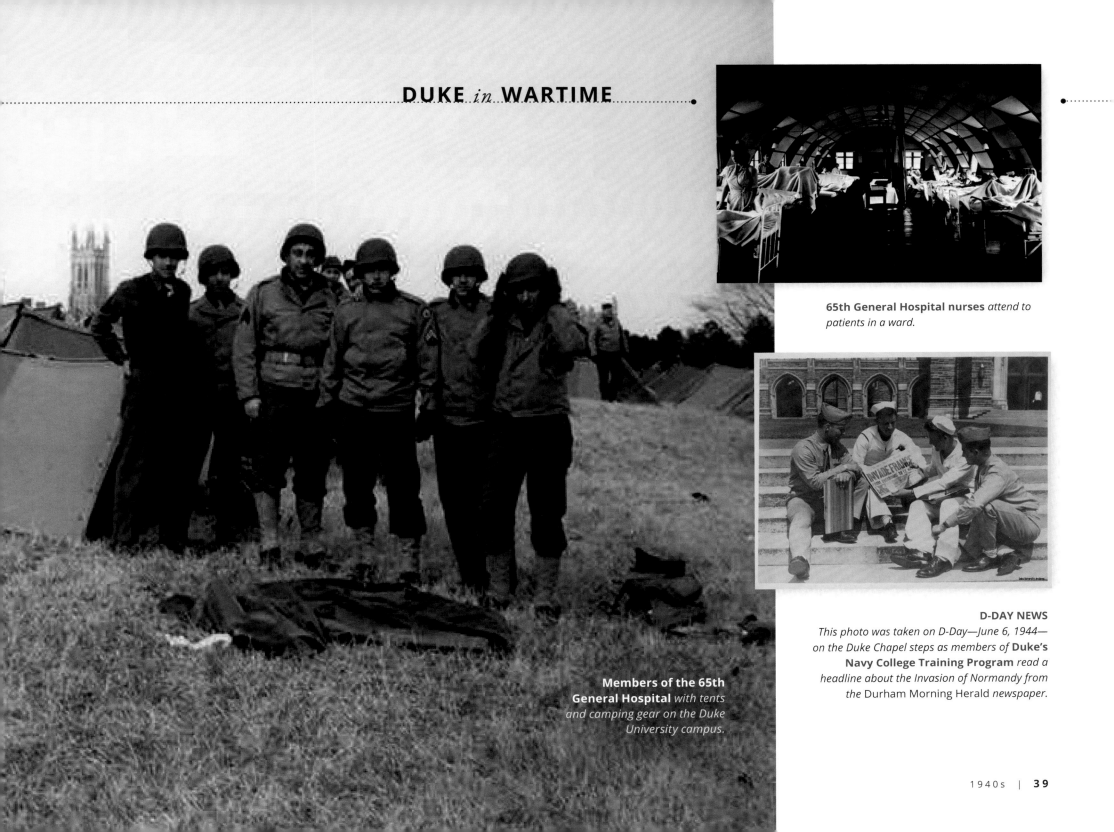

DUKE *in* WARTIME

65th General Hospital nurses *attend to patients in a ward.*

D-DAY NEWS
This photo was taken on D-Day—June 6, 1944—on the Duke Chapel steps as members of **Duke's Navy College Training Program** *read a headline about the Invasion of Normandy from the* Durham Morning Herald *newspaper.*

Members of the 65th General Hospital *with tents and camping gear on the Duke University campus.*

ROSE BOWL

THE ROSE BOWL *in* DURHAM

Duke fans were thrilled when Duke was invited to play Oregon State College in the 1942 Rose Bowl. But after Japan attacked Pearl Harbor on December 7, 1941, large sporting events on the West Coast were canceled for safety reasons. Duke football coach Wallace Wade proposed a solution: Duke could host the game in Durham. All parties agreed, and tickets, priced at $4.40, sold out in three days. Portable bleachers were loaned by neighboring universities—the University of North Carolina, North Carolina State University, and Wake Forest University—which increased the seating capacity of Duke's stadium from 35,000 to 56,000. On a rainy day and with a muddy field on January 1, 1942, Oregon State upset Duke 20–16.

For almost 80 years, it was the only time in the Rose Bowl's 100-year history that the game was played outside of Pasadena. Because of rising COVID-19 cases in Southern California in December 2020, the game was moved to AT&T Stadium in Arlington, Texas.

WALLACE WADE: COACH *and* COLONEL

Duke head football coach **Wallace Wade** was a notable leader in the United States war effort as well as on the football field. Wade had served as captain of cavalry of the 117th Infantry during World War I. Following the 1942 Rose Bowl game, at age 49, he signed up again to fight in World War II, while basketball coach Edmund Cameron took over Wade's football coaching duties.

Promoted to lieutenant colonel, Wade led the 272nd Army Field Artillery Battalion in 1944 into consequential battles, including the Battle of Normandy and the Battle of the Bulge, and was awarded a Bronze Star medal for his service. In 1945, he returned to Duke—first as director of athletics and then as head football coach.

1940s

*Aerial view of Duke Stadium during the **Rose Bowl, 1942**.*

ATHLETICS

Duke cheerleaders, *ca. 1943.*

Duke Indoor Stadium *opened on January 6, 1940, and was rededicated in 1972 as* **Cameron Indoor Stadium**, *named for longtime coach and Director of Athletics Eddie Cameron. The building had 8,800 seats, but standing room allowed total attendance to reach 9,500. Renovations in 1987–88 removed the standing room areas and added an electronic scoreboard and brass railings; air-conditioning was added in 2002.* Sports Illustrated *ranked Cameron Indoor Stadium fourth on its list of the top 20 sporting venues of the 20th century. Today, Cameron serves as the home venue for Duke men's basketball, women's basketball, volleyball, and wrestling.*

Members of the men's basketball team at North Carolina College for Negroes who participated in the **"Secret Game"** *were (left to right) Coach John B. McLendon, George Parks, George Lindsey "Crazy Horse" Samuels Jr., Billy Williams, James "Boogie" Hardy, Aubrey "Stinky" Stanley, Floyd "Cootie" Brown, Henry Wilson "Big Dog" Thomas, and team manager Edward "Pee Wee" Boyd.*

"THE SECRET GAME"

On Sunday morning, March 12, 1944, the basketball team of the Duke Medical School—which included several former college stars—drove across town to play an undercover game against the storied varsity squad of the North Carolina College for Negroes, which became **North Carolina Central University**. *The game, played for bragging rights of the best team in Durham, was illegal during the Jim Crow era, and neither the NCAA nor the National Invitation Tournament (NIT) allowed for intercollegiate competition between historically white and historically Black universities. The final score: North Carolina College 88, Duke Medical School 44. The remarkable story was uncovered and written by historian Scott Ellsworth A.M.'77, Ph.D.'82, first in the* New York Times Magazine, *then in* Duke Magazine, *and later as a book,* The Secret Game: A Wartime Story of Courage, Change, and Basketball's Lost Triumph.

The **Duke Medical School's** *squad included (left to right) Dick Thistlewaite, Homer Seiber, Dave Hubbell, Harry Wechsler, Ed Johnson, Dick Symmonds, John McCoy, and Jack Burgess.*

Robert Lee Flowers *was first hired as a professor of electrical engineering and mathematics by Trinity College. In 1891, he wired the new buildings at the new Trinity College campus in Durham for electricity. He served Duke for over 60 years, holding the positions of treasurer, vice president, and chancellor as well as president.*

George Wall.

GEORGE *and* GEORGE-FRANK WALL

In 1946, longtime Duke employee George-Frank Wall made a bequest to Duke of $100. His family had a long connection to Duke: George-Frank Wall's father, George Wall, was a formerly enslaved person who was hired by Trinity College president Braxton Craven in Randolph County in 1870. When the college moved to Durham in 1892, George Wall also made the move. With his wife, he would later buy land near the new campus and became a leader in his neighborhood, which was later named Walltown in his honor.

George-Frank Wall, the oldest of George Wall's nine children, grew up in Durham and worked at Duke as a janitor until his death in 1953. A conscientious worker, he was well known and respected by students and administrators. In his will in 1946, he made a $100 gift to Duke, which was added to the scholarship fund. Of course, this was a time when no Black students were admitted to the university. He also named President Robert Flowers as the executor of his estate.

In the years since, Duke has forged strong partnerships with the Walltown neighborhood, including the Walltown Neighborhood Clinic, which provides accessible and affordable healthcare services to Durham residents.

In 2024, the Duke University Board of Trustees approved a proposal from President Vincent Price to rename the East Campus Union, home of the Marketplace and the Trinity Café, as the

George-Frank Wall, *1946.*

George and George-Frank Wall Center for Student Life. In the announcement, President Price said, "Naming [the East Union] in honor of the Walls acknowledges the important role they played, and that generations of housekeeping and dining staff members have played, in nurturing our campus community and creating a supportive environment for students throughout Duke's history." ■

WOMEN *in* ACADEMIA

Juanita Kreps, *Ph.D., an Appalachian coal miner's daughter, earned her Ph.D. in economics from Duke in 1948 and joined the Duke faculty in 1955. Later named James B. Duke Professor of Economics, she served as dean of the Woman's College, associate provost, and vice president. In 1976 she became the first woman to serve as U.S. secretary of commerce.*

Alice Mary Baldwin *was a Duke historian who served as dean of the Woman's College from 1923 until her retirement in 1947. Baldwin Auditorium is named in her honor. She is pictured above receiving an honorary degree from Duke in 1949.*

Engineering students, *ca. 1943.*

INAUGURATION

President Hollis Edens, 1949

The son of a Methodist minister from Tennessee, Edens (top right) came to Duke with a doctorate in public administration from Harvard and administrative experience from the University System of Georgia and the Rockefeller Foundation.

*Marine scientist **Harold J. Humm**, Ph.D., director of the **Duke Marine Laboratory** in Beaufort, N.C., waits in the water to have his diving helmet fitted over his head. At least 11 species of marine organisms have been named in Humm's honor.*

1950s | A DECADE *in* RETROSPECT

50

Duke pediatrician Jay Arena, M.D., leads the push for drug companies to develop the child-proof safety cap for medicine bottles

▼

51

Hanes House, a dormitory and teaching facility for nurses, opens

In Duke Indoor Stadium, men's basketball plays against Temple, which starts a Black player, Sam Sylvester; it's believed to be the first integrated game in the South

▼

52

University Council, a faculty advisory committee, established

Estelle Flowers Spears, a 1914 graduate of Trinity College, becomes the first woman elected as a trustee

53

James B. Duke Professorships created, funded by The Duke Endowment

Duke becomes a charter member of the Atlantic Coast Conference (ACC)

54

55

56

57

58

59

Main administrative building *opens and is named in honor of George G. Allen, close adviser to James B. Duke and president of The Duke Endowment*

Duke Poison Control Center *opens—the second such center in the United States*

Men's Graduate Center *(now Trent Hall) opens*

Duke University Union *is created*

Duke Center for Aging *created*

Ella Fountain Pratt *is hired to develop arts programs at Duke*

Duke student-athlete Dave Sime named "the world's fastest human"

Flowers Building *is renovated and renamed for President Robert Flowers*

The name Duke University Medical Center is used for the School of Medicine and Hospital

The Duke University Golf Club, *designed by Robert Trent Jones Sr., opens to the public with President Edens hitting the first ball off the No. 1 tee at the dedication event*

Wannamaker residence hall *opens*

Elizabeth Hanford Dole *graduates from the Woman's College; she later served as Secretary of Transportation and Secretary of Labor and represented North Carolina in the United States Senate*

Research Triangle Park *(RTP) established*

The Duke School of Medicine *adds its signature third year of research into the medical curriculum*

Then-U.S. senator John F. Kennedy speaks at Duke

Senator John F. Kennedy *in the Flowers Building on West Campus before his address in Page Auditorium, December 2, 1959. Kennedy would announce that he was running for president one month later.*

*Comedian Bob Hope entertained Duke students at **"Joe College" weekend** in 1951.*

S 'n' S presents
"Joe College" Weekend
featuring
THE 'SENTIMENTAL JOURNEY' MAN
LES BROWN
AND HIS BAND
OF RENOWN

50s

Bob Pascal '56 was an All-America running back at Duke who helped lead his team to three ACC championships and a 34–7 win over Nebraska in the Orange Bowl on January 1, 1955. Pascal was inducted into the Duke Athletics Hall of Fame in 1995 and was a loyal supporter of the football program. The **Pascal Field House** at Duke is named in his honor.

On September 29, 1951, the Duke football team played Pittsburgh in the first nationally televised live sporting event. The game was broadcast across the country—"coast to coast"—on NBC. The Blue Devils won 19–14, signaling an arrival on the national stage.

Arthur Hollis Edens was president of Duke for the entire decade of the 1950s. A former professor of political science, Edens maintained the commitment to academic freedom that had been a hallmark of the institution since its Trinity College days. This commitment was put to the test when a Duke sociologist, **Hornell Hart**, Ph.D., published a study of Senator Joseph McCarthy's Senate hearings about communists in the U.S. State Department. McCarthy threatened legal action against Duke, demanding that the university suppress the research. Duke supported the professor, and President Edens replied: "It is axiomatic in University circles that a professor has the right to pursue research investigations of his choice."

Professors may have had academic freedom in the 1950s, but freedoms for women students were limited. Women had strict rules for curfew and were required to obtain permission and "sign out" before going off campus. Duke women were expected to wear dresses and skirts on campus, with "hats, hose, and heels" for services in Duke Chapel. A 1950 pamphlet produced by the Women's Student Government admonished incoming students: "We are Duke coeds wherever we go.

We represent Duke University and its standards of conduct on the campus, in Durham, on visits, and at home."

By the mid-1950s, Duke's all-white student body grew more supportive of desegregation. Both the men's and women's student governments passed resolutions calling on the Board of Trustees to desegregate the university—a step that would not be taken until the 1960s.

President Edens's strategy to advance the university was to invest in Duke's existing strengths. Under his leadership, Duke expanded enrollment, increased faculty salaries, and developed graduate programs. Fundraising enabled Duke to grow and achieve national prominence in selected areas. From The Duke Endowment in the 1950s came significant gifts to recognize academic excellence, creating the James B. Duke Professorships to honor distinguished scholars across the Duke academic community, as well as the James B. Duke Fellowships for graduate study. In the decades since, the fellowships have supported hundreds of talented Duke Ph.D. students.

At the same time, the federal government was making strategic investments as part of the postwar boom in public support for higher education. Founded in 1955, the Duke Center for the Study of Aging and Human Development was funded in 1957 by the National Institutes of Health, along with four other U.S. centers on aging.

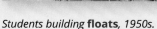
*Students building **floats**, 1950s.*

*"**Joe College**" started in 1951 as a weekend in the spring with music, dancing, and a parade with floats. This popular tradition was considered "the highlight of the social year" and featured performances from Duke alumnus **Les Brown** '36 and His Band of Renown to Duke Ellington to Linda Ronstadt.*

Chairman of Duke's psychiatry department and founding director **Ewald W. "Bud" Busse**, M.D., tapped into Duke's growing interest in interdisciplinary research and forged connections between the Medical Center and the rest of the university. As of 2024, the Duke Aging Center is the longest continuously funded aging center in the nation and continues its legacy of excellence in research, teaching, and clinical care.

Another notable Duke leader in the 1950s was **Marcus Hobbs**, Ph.D. A triple Duke alumnus, Hobbs joined the chemistry department in 1936 and spent his entire career at Duke, serving as chair of the chemistry department, dean of the graduate school, dean of the university, and eventually as provost. He led the creation in 1951 of the Office of Ordnance Research at Duke, which later became the U.S. Army Research Office (Durham). Hobbs was honored with the University Medal for Distinguished Meritorious service in 1989 for the way he "strongly influenced the crucial middle years of this institution's development as a university."

Hobbs was also instrumental in the development of the Research Triangle Park (RTP). The RTP website provides this context: "In the 1950s, North Carolina was in economic decline. Ranked 47th out of 48 in the nation in per capita income, the state was a Southern economy dependent on tobacco, textiles and furniture manufacturing. University graduates were leaving the state in droves in search of better jobs."

Tapped by Governor Luther Hodges to be part of an exploratory committee, Hobbs compiled the scientific research being conducted at Duke, North Carolina State University, and UNC-Chapel Hill and helped to envision a collaboration between the three universities that would attract companies that could draw on their intellectual resources. The nation's first successful research park, RTP now includes more than 260 private, governmental research, and nonprofit companies in technology, pharmaceuticals, and finance on 7,000 acres. Companies in RTP employ more than 50,000 people, making the region one of the nation's leading centers for research, science, and engineering with one of the highest concentrations of Ph.D.s and M.D.s in the world. ∎

*East Campus **Dope Shop**.*

1950s

William J. Griffith, *who graduated from Duke in 1950, was named director of the student union in 1954. Over the next four decades, Bill Griffith was a devoted university administrator and a beloved mentor to generations of Duke students as the university evolved and changed. He helped make the Duke Student Union a national model for cultivating student leadership. Griffith also helped to advise the Duke student government, Project WILD, the Community Service Center, the Women's Center, the Black Student Alliance, the Career Development Center, Counseling and Psychological Services, the Publications Board, and other student groups and services. The William J. Griffith University Service Award and the Griffith Film Theater in the Bryan Center are named in his honor.*

1950s DUKE WOMEN

Despite the social restrictions, women in the 1950s deeply valued the academic experience at Duke. **Trustee Emerita Sally Dalton Robinson '55** majored in history, was elected to Phi Beta Kappa, and served as president of her sophomore class in the Woman's College. In 2005, Sally Robinson served as co-chair of the **Financial Aid Initiative,** which raised more than $300 million in new endowment for financial aid. Robinson recalled in a 2019 interview that she had followed Duke football on the radio since childhood and knew she wanted to go to Duke:

"Those four years, the intellectual life that Duke provided for me, was amazing, and I loved it. . . . I remember one time, I was driving between East and West Campus, and it suddenly hit me that all the courses that I'd been taking that year—whether it was history, philosophy, art, literature—that they were all connected. And that was a great moment for me, and it just made me so grateful for the liberal arts education that Duke gave me."

Cinderella float, *May 1959.*

Late night study session, 1951.

Twenty-three years ago the social standards committee of the Woman's College had its beginnings. Its purpose was two-fold: first, that it adopt certain standards to become an integral part of the life of Duke women; and second, that it promote enjoyable social activity on the campus.

This handbook is designed primarily to answer some of the most common questions, and a few of those not so common, which confront you, a new Duchess. You will find here answers to some of the vital questions which trouble so many: what to wear, what to do, where to go, and what to expect under certain circumstances. We are Duke coeds wherever we go. We represent Duke University and its standards of conduct on the campus, in Durham, on visits, and at home.

We who have been here know the charm of life at Duke, and we want you to know it, too. You will feel that you *belong* the minute you arrive—Duke spirit is like that.

Social Standards Committee 1950-1951

Social Standards Regulations
1950-1951

On Campus:
1. Coats must be worn over gym clothes on campus.
2. Jackets must be worn over sunback dresses on campus, to the Union, and to classes.
3. There is no walking or sitting on the grass of the main quadrangles.
4. There is no talking out of the windows of residence houses.
5. There is no talking, writing, or studying in assembly.

To the Union:
1. Blue jeans may be worn to breakfast only when a field trip follows. Coats must be worn over them.
2. Gym clothes are never worn to the Union.
3. Students must dress for breakfast—no pajamas. These rules also apply to Southgate.
4. Hose are worn to the Union on Sunday at noon.

Sunbathing:
1. Coeds may sunbathe only in the section of the campus behind the gym which is designated for that purpose. Bathing suits or play suits must be worn when sunbathing.
2. Shirts and shorts are proper attire on the tennis courts.

Off Campus:
1. Shorts are not worn on cabin parties.
2. Blue jeans are not worn off campus after a cabin party.
3. Students must wear hose downtown to dinner on Saturday and Sunday evenings.
4. Formals may be worn to dinner at approved places before a formal dance is attended.
5. Hats and hose are worn to church.
6. Blue jeans may be worn without coats on field trips; however, they may not be worn on campus or to the Union afterwards.

[12]

*This pamphlet, published by the **Women's Student Government Social Standards Committee**, set out strict rules for dress and behavior for women students. These rules were in addition to the regulations in the official Woman's College Handbook produced by the university. Women students took an exam testing their knowledge of the rules during Orientation Week.*

Duke Forestry *students, 1950s.*

Marine ecology class, **Duke University Marine Lab**, *1952.*

SQUARE DANCING
at the IIE's Summer Orientation, 1953

Through the **Institute for International Education,** *the U.S. State Department sponsored programs for international students. From 1950 to 1957, Duke hosted a summer IIE orientation program for students coming from abroad to study in the United States.*

*Duke Jewish students at **Hillel Shabbat** meeting at Duke's Divinity School, 1954 or 1955. (left to right) Unidentified Duke student, Marvin Marx, Bob Nolan, Chick Becker, Saul Bendayan, Howard Block, and Bernie Goldstein.*

JEWISH LIFE *at* DUKE

*Jewish students have been part of the Duke community since it was Trinity College. Class of 1958 alumna **Charlene Nachman Waldman** shared the following reflection in 2010 about Jewish life at Duke in the 1950s:*

"Jewish students at Duke in the 1950s would not have imagined that one day there would be a Freeman Center for Jewish Life providing religious services, great food, holiday celebrations, educational programs, trips, and other wonderful opportunities.

But there was Jewish life! Students led Shabbat services every Friday evening in a room in the Divinity School. A special banner covered a cross in the room.

Every two months Hillel sponsored a bagel breakfast. My cousin Charles (Chick) Becker '56 remembers ordering the food from a deli in Baltimore and picking the food up at the Durham bus station. Rabbi Efe Rosenzweig, the rabbi for North Carolina Hillel, attended the bagel breakfasts.

Jewish students engaged with the Durham Jewish community in many ways. Students were welcome at Beth El Synagogue for the High Holidays. I remember attending a Yom Kippur breakfast at the rabbi's home.

The Evans family in Durham were very hospitable to Jewish students. Mutt Evans was mayor of Durham for many years and his wife Sarah was very active in regional and national Jewish activities. They invited Jewish students to their home for celebrations of holidays and special occasions such as graduation. . . .

The fraternities ZBT and AEPi and the sorority AEPhi were important aspects of Jewish life.

In the broader community, Jewish students were leaders in many ways. Nolan Rogers '53 was student body president in the academic year 1952–53 and was captain of the Duke lacrosse team. Mike Temko '58 was president of the Inter Fraternity Council and Sally Kraus '58 led the Women's Panhellenic Council. . . . .

Duke students are very lucky to have the Freeman Center, and we were also lucky for the Jewish life we experienced at Duke." ∎

1950s

DINK, 1957

For much of the 20th century, students entering Duke were required to wear distinctive headgear to identify them as first-years: men wore dinks (first a beanie and later a floppy hat), while women wore bows in their hair. If Duke won the annual Duke–UNC football game, the freshmen could ditch their dinks and bows—but if Duke lost, the freshmen were stuck wearing their dinks and bows for the entire first semester.

Freshmen **bows**.

Freshman move-in *day, ca. 1956.*

First-year women learn the tradition of **"The Sower" statue** *on East Campus: Strolling couples would place pennies in the statue's hand, and, as former University Archivist Tim Pyatt explained in* Duke Magazine *in 2009, "if the coins were gone the next time the couple returned, the gentleman could claim a kiss."*

Freshmen at **University House**, *the former residence of Benjamin N. Duke that was later used by the university as an events space.*

ATHLETIC LEGENDS

In the 1950s, Duke track & field star **Dave Sime** A.B. '58, M.D. '62 was known as "the world's fastest human." Sports Illustrated called him "Superman in spikes" after he set seven world records. While an injury kept him out of the 1956 Olympic games, he won a silver medal in the 1960 Olympics in Rome. Sime (pronounced Sim) came to Duke on a baseball scholarship, but when he began to work out informally with the track team to stay in shape for baseball, his superb speed was immediately noticed by Duke track & field coach Al Buehler, who began preparing Sime to compete internationally.

Sime was named the Atlantic Coast Conference (ACC) Athlete of the Year in 1956; he was also a first-team All-Conference selection in baseball. Duke later named him the university's most outstanding athlete of the 20th century.

After graduating from Duke, Sime enrolled in the Duke University School of Medicine, graduating with honors. He completed his internship in ophthalmology at Duke and practiced medicine for 40 years in Miami, where he became a leading specialist in eye surgery and intraocular lens implants.

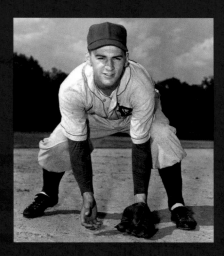

Dick Groat '52 was a two-sport star at Duke, earning All-America honors in both baseball and basketball in 1951 and 1952. In his senior year, Groat was the National Player of the Year in basketball—and on the baseball diamond, he posted a career batting average of .375 and led the Blue Devils to their first College World Series appearance. When his basketball jersey (#10) was retired as a surprise at his last baseball game, he was the first Duke athlete to receive this honor in any sport.

After graduating from Duke, Groat had a 14-year professional baseball career that saw him win World Series titles with the Pittsburgh Pirates in 1960 and the St. Louis Cardinals in 1964. He was inducted in 1975 to the Duke Athletics Hall of Fame.

MEDICINE and TECHNOLOGY

The **Duke Center for the Study of Aging and Human Development** *was established in 1955. Here, psychological testing in gerontology is administered, January 1958.*

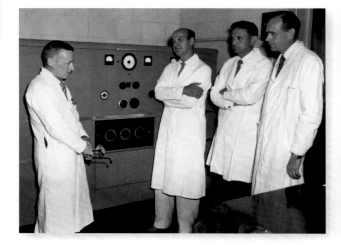

Leaders in Duke Medicine are pictured by an ultracentrifuge in September 1957.

(Left to right) **Barnes Woodhall**, *M.D., chief of neurosurgery, 1937–60, and chancellor of Duke Hospital, 1960–64, established the first brain tumor program in the nation in 1937;* **Philip Handler**, *Ph.D., James B. Duke Professor and chair of Biochemistry, served as president of the National Academy of Sciences from 1969 to 1981 and was honored with the National Medal of Science in 1981;* **Ewald W. Busse**, *M.D., founding director of the Duke University Center for the Study of Aging and Human Development, later served as president of the International Association of Gerontology;* **Eugene A. Stead Jr.**, *M.D., chair of the Department of Medicine from 1947 to 1967, established the first formal physician assistant training program in the nation in 1965.*

1950s

The term **"Duke University Medical Center"** was first used in 1957 to designate the combined facilities for medical and nursing instruction, treatment, and research. Duke began to develop advances in heart surgery, including the use of deep hypothermia during open-heart surgery.

1960s | A DECADE *in* RETROSPECT

60

President Edens resigns, Paul Gross removed as chief academic officer—a turn of events known as the "Gross-Edens affair"

▲ **J. Deryl Hart,** *M.D., becomes Duke's fourth president*

Robert Taylor Cole, *Ph.D., becomes Duke's first provost*

61

The Duke University Board of Trustees announces the integration of the university's graduate and professional schools

Walter Thaniel Johnson Jr. *and* **David Robinson** *are the first Black students to enroll in Duke Law School;* **Ruben Lee Speaks** *is the first Black student to enroll in Duke Divinity School*

Anne Firor Scott, *Ph.D., joins the Department of History; she would help establish the field of women's history*

62

▲ *School of Law moves into its new building*

Academic Council *formed*

The Board of Trustees *announces that undergraduate students will be admitted without regard to race*

October 26, Ray Charles performs in Duke Indoor Stadium

63

Wilhelmina Reuben-Cooke, Mary Mitchell Harris, Gene Kendall, Cassandra Smith Rush, *and* **Nathaniel White Jr.** *enroll at Duke; they are Duke's first Black undergraduate students*

William Griffith *becomes dean of student affairs, a post he holds until 1991*

64

65

66

67

68

69

The Rev. Dr.
Martin Luther
King Jr. *visits Duke
and speaks in Page
Auditorium*

William Anlyan,
*M.D., becomes
chancellor for
health affairs*

Douglas M.
Knight, *Ph.D.,
becomes Duke's
fifth president*

*Duke establishes
the nation's first*
Physician Assistant
program

The Parapsychology
Laboratory *closes*

The Triangle
Universities
Nuclear Laboratory
opens at Duke

Local 77 established
*as Duke's first labor
union*

Samuel DuBois Cook,
*Ph.D., hired by the
Department of Political
Science, is Duke's first Black
faculty member*

The Duke Medical
Scientist Training
Program, *a joint degree
program leading to both the
M.D. and the Ph.D. degrees,
is founded—one of the first
three in the nation*

Duke University Primate
Center *is founded, known
today as the Duke Lemur
Center*

Anthony Oyewole, *an
international student from
Nigeria, transfers to Duke
in 1964 as a junior and
graduates in 1966, becoming
the first Black person to earn
a Duke degree; he would
also earn a Ph.D. from Duke
in political science in 1970*

*The Men's Student
Government Association
and the Women's
Student Government
Association merge to
form the* Associated
Students of Duke
University (ASDU)

April 5–11,
Silent Vigil

Fred Black *and*
Sylvia Sloan *are the
first Black couple to
marry in Duke Chapel*

The undergraduate
curriculum
*undergoes its first
major revision since
the 1920s*

Students protest
Dow Chemical
Company *during a
job recruiting visit
to Duke because
of the company's
association with the
use of napalm in the
Vietnam War*

Perkins Library *opens*

March 1, Janis Joplin
performs at Duke

April 26, Aretha
Franklin *performs at
Duke*

February 13, Allen
Building takeover

School of Business
Administration *is
founded*

Museum of Art *opens*

Douglas Knight *resigns*

19

N, DICK, & HARRY WELCOME JOANNE, JUDY, & MARSHA!

Judy
YEA CLASS
ΦΔΘ of '67
ΔΔΔ
Bar-B-Q

Duke
Gardens
April 28

60s

J. Deryl Hart *served as president of Duke University from 1960 to 1963. Previously, he was professor and chair of the Department of Surgery at Duke. Hart's home on Duke University Road, called Hart House, now serves as the official residence of Duke's president.*

The 1960s were a decade of profound social change in America—and at Duke. With the Civil Rights Movement, the Vietnam War and antiwar protests, and the cultural revolution sweeping the country, the 1960s drew Duke students, faculty, and staff into passionate engagement with the world and with each other.

The decade began at Duke with administrative turmoil and controversy. President A. Hollis Edens and Vice President of Education Paul Gross held different visions for the future of Duke, and feeling under pressure from some trustees, Edens announced his resignation in February 1960. Shortly thereafter, Paul Gross, who was serving as the university's chief academic officer, was dismissed by the Board of Trustees. The announcements filled the campus with shock and confusion.

The departures led to the creation of the office of the provost, first held by **R. Taylor Cole**, Ph.D., and the establishment of the Academic Council, Duke's faculty senate. Today, faculty and administrators are proud of Duke's strong culture of shared governance.

J. Deryl Hart, chair of the Department of Surgery and a longtime leader in the School of Medicine, served as Duke's president from 1960 to 1963. During this time, he increased faculty salaries, doubled the number of distinguished professorships, and improved the Offices of the Registrar, Undergraduate Admissions, and Development. Most significantly, he presided over the opening of Duke's doors for the first time to Black students.

◄ Wilhelmina Reuben-Cooke, Nathaniel White Jr., and Mary Mitchell Harris graduated from Duke in 1967.

Beginning in 1948, students and faculty had petitioned the university to desegregate. On March 8, 1961, the Duke University Board of Trustees announced that students would be admitted to the university's graduate and professional schools "without regard to race, creed, or national origin," effective September 1, 1961. That fall, **Walter Thaniel Johnson Jr.** and **David Robinson** were the first Black students to enroll in Duke Law School, while **Ruben Lee Speaks** was the first Black student to enroll in Duke Divinity School. They arrived at a Duke campus that still bore the evidence of segregation, including a section at the football stadium designated "colored."

On June 2, 1962, the Board of Trustees announced that undergraduate students would be admitted without regard to race. The decision was regarded as even more consequential than the integration of the graduate and professional schools, as it would integrate the residence halls. Students and faculty overwhelmingly cheered the resolution. However, as President **Douglas M. Knight** would later write in his 1989 book *Street of Dreams*, "This was not a unanimous decision; there were abstentions from the vote, and a good deal of silent unhappiness among alumni and others in the region."

In 1963, the first five Black undergraduates enrolled at Duke: **Wilhelmina Reuben-Cooke, Mary Mitchell Harris, Gene Kendall, Cassandra Smith Rush**, and **Nathaniel White Jr.** Joining a university with no Black faculty or administrators, they found that many Black

*In February 1969, the General Library and its new addition reopened with a new name, **Perkins Library**. Named for William R. Perkins, trustee of The Duke Endowment, the new building had five times the space of the original building.*

*In preparation for the **reopening of the library**, more than 800 volunteers from Duke fraternities spent their weekends moving more than one million books to the new building. An incentive of $1,000 was offered to the group who contributed the most hours; **Sigma Phi Epsilon** won the prize.*

campus workers took pride in their arrival on campus and made special efforts to support them and connect them to churches and communities in Durham.

Samuel DuBois Cook was hired in 1966 by Duke's political science department. He became Duke's first Black faculty member—and one of the first at a predominantly white Southern university. Cook later became president of Dillard University in New Orleans and a trustee of Duke University. At Duke, the Samuel DuBois Cook Center on Social Equity and the Samuel DuBois Cook Society and Awards are named in his honor.

Throughout the 1960s, as on many American college campuses, Duke students protested the injustices they saw in society. In 1962, white students from Duke and the University of North Carolina joined Durham's Black students to protest and eventually boycott the segregated Sears Roebuck, Walgreens, and the Carolina Theatre in Durham. That summer, Durham's movie theaters were desegregated. Duke students also protested the Vietnam War on campus in the 1960s and '70s.

Duke continued to grow and expand in other ways in the 1960s. In 1963, the School of Law moved into its new building, with U.S. Supreme Court Chief Justice Earl Warren speaking at the dedication ceremony.

In 1965, Eugene A. Stead Jr., then-chairman of the Department of Medicine, started the Physician Assistant educational program at Duke—the first in the nation. The program was designed to address a need for more medical practitioners and provide a meaningful career pathway for former military corpsmen that could draw on their experience.

The next year, the Duke University Primate Center was founded through a collaboration between two researchers: John Buettner-Janusch, Ph.D., of Yale and Duke biologist **Peter Klopfer**, Ph.D. A colony of lemurs was relocated from Connecticut to a site cleared in Duke Forest, two miles from West Campus. Today, the Duke Lemur Center houses more than 200 primates, including lemurs, lorises, and tarsiers, across 13 species—more than anywhere in the world outside of Madagascar—and its non-invasive scientific research has made the Center a global authority on lemur genetics, conservation, and veterinary medicine.

In 1968, the undergraduate curriculum underwent its first major revision since the 1920s. The Krueger Report, led by **Robert Krueger**, D.Phil., an assistant professor of English, and based on a survey of students and alumni, emphasized the importance of seminar-style discussion, independent study and research, and interdisciplinary and experiential learning. Duke's "New Curriculum" reduced the standard academic load from five courses to four and established Program II, which allowed students to design their own majors.

Following the assassination of the Rev. Dr. Martin Luther King Jr. on April 4, 1968, Duke students were galvanized into action, and around 250 students marched to President Douglas M. Knight's home. That group was later joined by hundreds more for the Silent Vigil on the main quad on West Campus. The vigil had strict rules to maintain solemnity, and some professors held classes on the quad in solidarity. The vigil focused on protesting Duke's discriminatory policies and advocated for better wages and working conditions for the housekeepers, janitors, and dining hall workers. The administration agreed to salary increases for the workers by the conclusion of the vigil on April 11.

Students kept up the pressure on other key issues on campus.

In October, Black students presented the administration with 12 points of concern, including the still low numbers of Black students and faculty members at Duke, as well as the fact that some university officials continued to maintain their memberships in segregated facilities.

Early 1969 saw incremental progress: President Knight withdrew from Durham's segregated country club, and the Academic Council formed a committee to address the student demands. Nonetheless, students remained frustrated.

In the early morning of February 13, 1969, 60 members of the Afro-American Society entered the Allen Building, Duke's main administration building, and issued their demands to the university. The students held conversations with faculty and administrators but were not able to reach a resolution.

Over the course of the long, tense day, dozens of Durham city police and other law enforcement who had been called in by the administration amassed around the building, with National Guard troops on standby off campus. A large crowd of white students also gathered on the quad to show support for the Black students inside the building. Eventually the Black students departed the Allen Building peacefully. At the same time, police in riot gear stormed the building, engaged the crowd with tear gas and clubs, and made arrests.

The Allen Building takeover, as it became known, led to the resignation of President Knight. The event elicited many different reactions from the Duke community: students were mostly sympathetic, while many alumni were not. The incident provoked a response that ultimately strengthened the university and launched important academic and administrative programs that are points of pride today, including the creation of the Black Studies program and establishment of the Office of Black Affairs. ■

The Rev. Dr. Martin Luther King Jr. *visited Duke on November 17, 1964, and spoke about the progress of the Civil Rights Movement to a crowd that filled Page Auditorium and overflowed into the wooded area just outside the building.*

1960s EXPANSION

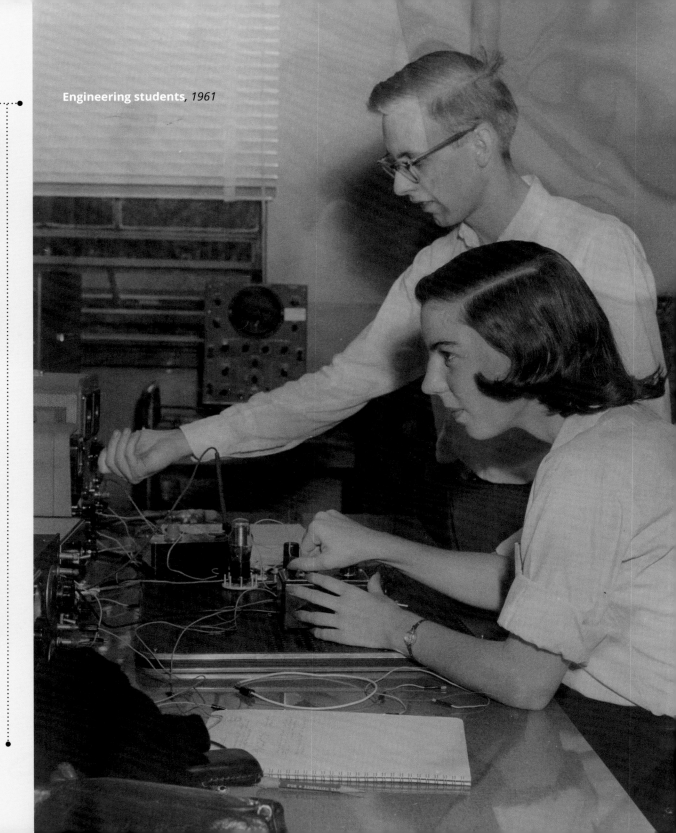

Established in 1968 with funds from the National Science Foundation, the **Phytotron** is a controlled environment research facility housing 68 plant growth chambers and six controlled greenhouses.

The Science Building on East Campus was renovated in 1969 to become the home for the **Museum of Art.** After the Nasher Museum of Art opened at Duke, the building was remodeled again and was named in 2008 for Ernestine P. Friedl, former chair of the Department of Anthropology and dean of Trinity College of Arts and Sciences.

Engineering students, 1961

*The **Duke University Primate Center** was established in 1966. Today, the Duke Lemur Center is an internationally acclaimed non-invasive research center housing over 200 lemurs and bush babies across 13 species—the most diverse population of lemurs on Earth outside their native Madagascar. The center is open to the public and welcomes more than 35,000 visitors annually to its location on 80 wooded acres.*

*The **School of Business Administration** was established in 1969. Today, the **Fuqua School of Business** is a top-ranked graduate business school that attracts and develops leaders who bring out the strengths of people and organizations. Fuqua currently enrolls more than 2,000 students a year in a wide range of degree programs. In the Daytime MBA Class of 2024, 48 percent of students are women, and 43 percent of the class identify as minority students. The Class of 2024 represents 55 different countries, with 39 percent of students holding international citizenship.*

Duke's primate facility hosts 15 species

Primates vital in research projects

By Richard Smurthwaite

PIONEERS

62

Matthew A. Zimmerman *enrolled in* **Duke Divinity School** *in 1962 and in 1965 became Duke's first Black M.Div. graduate. A major general in the U.S. Army, he served as the 18th Chief of Chaplains of the Army—the first Black person to hold this position.*

James Eaton, Ida Stephens Owens *(Physiology Ph.D.'67), and* **Odell Richardson Reuben** *(Religion Ph.D.'69) are the first Black students to enroll in the Graduate School of Arts and Sciences.*

63

Five Black undergraduates enter as first-year students: **Wilhelmina Reuben-Cooke, Mary Mitchell Harris, Gene Kendall, Cassandra Smith Rush,** *and* **Nathaniel White Jr.**

◄

W. Delano Meriwether *M.D.'67 is the first Black student to enroll in Duke's School of Medicine.*

▼

61

Ruben Lee Speaks *is the first Black student to enroll in Duke Divinity School.*

Walter Thaniel Johnson Jr. *J.D.'64 and* **David Robinson II** *J.D.'64 are the first Black students to enroll in Duke Law School.*

65

Claudius B. "C.B." Claiborne *'69 matriculated to Duke University on a presidential scholarship. He played for a year on the freshman basketball team (NCAA rules prohibited freshmen on varsity teams at the time), becoming Duke's first Black student-athlete. He then joined the varsity men's basketball team for the 1966–67 season.*

67

Donna Allen Harris *B.S.N.'71 is Duke's first Black nursing student.*

Nathaniel White Jr. *'67 grew up in Durham, where he was a star student at the then-segregated Hillside High School. Although his family lived only three miles from campus, he said that going to Duke was "like going to a whole new city." He later recalled: "In August of 1963, I was in the March on Washington. . . . Within a week of that, I was starting my classes at Duke."*

*In 1967, **Wilhelmina Reuben-Cooke** was elected May Queen. While some alumni objected, the title signaled the respect Reuben-Cooke had earned from her peers in the Woman's College.*

Wilhelmina Reuben-Cooke '67 was one of the first five Black undergraduates to enroll at Duke in 1963. She was elected to Phi Beta Kappa and was chosen as May Queen. After graduating from Duke, Reuben-Cooke went on to a distinguished career as an attorney, professor of law, and senior administrator at Syracuse University and the University of the District of Columbia. She served as a member of the Duke University Board of Trustees from 1989 to 2001 and served as a trustee of The Duke Endowment until her passing in 2019. In 2021, Duke renamed and dedicated the Sociology-Psychology Building on West Campus as the Reuben-Cooke Building in her honor. Reuben-Cooke was interviewed by Bridget Booher '80 in the September–October 1992 issue of Duke Magazine:

"When I decided to come to Duke, I knew it wouldn't be an easy task. The majority of students were from the South, and most of them had never dealt with African Americans as peers. I assumed my social life wouldn't be great, and I knew my expectations about college would be tempered by reality. But I had a sense of personal commitment; it was the sixties and the quest for change and civil rights was gaining momentum. It seemed to all of us that we had a role to play.

What I discovered was that I never had any regrets [about choosing Duke]. I was socially active and had a lot of friends. And an important part of that experience was being forced to meet people and to develop relationships that I probably wouldn't have made in another context. That created in me a sense of optimism about the ways people can grow and change." ■

VOICES

SAMUEL DUBOIS COOK *and the* SILENT VIGIL

The Silent Vigil took place on the quad after the assassination of Rev. Dr. Martin Luther King Jr. It was a symbol of mourning and an effort to improve wages and working conditions for Duke's hourly workers.

Samuel DuBois Cook was Duke's first Black faculty member. In 1968, he was an associate professor of political science and a popular teacher on campus. Cook had been a university classmate of Dr. King and attended his funeral in Atlanta. When he returned to Duke after the funeral, he spoke to the students assembled on the quad for the Silent Vigil: "I do not know if you fully realize the ultimate significance of what you are doing. You would, of course, expect the victims of oppression to sacrifice, to take the hot sun, to take the rain, to sleep at night in the open and cold air, to expose their health, to do everything possible to remove the yoke of oppression and injustice. But you do not expect people born of privilege to undergo this harsh treatment. This is one of the things I think will help to redeem this country and help to create the beloved community. . . . You are making profound history."

He later reflected: "My own view is that the Silent Vigil was a noble event and a sacred or divine experience—historical, institutional, symbolic, existential, and personal. It was one of those supreme and unforgettable mountaintop experiences in which the 'Word was made flesh' . . . a transcendent moment and indelible memory."

Professor Cook later served as president of Dillard University in New Orleans for 22 years, returning to Duke to serve as a trustee. At Duke, the Samuel DuBois Cook Center on Social Equity and the Samuel DuBois Cook Society are named in his honor. ∎

JOIN US FOR THE DURATION

Check in with a monitor up front

WE SHALL NCT BE MOVED

SUPPORT THE VIGIL

The Silent Vigil, *including a march from West to East Campus, was a silent demonstration at Duke University, April 5–11, 1968, following the assassination of Dr. Martin Luther King Jr. Up to 1,400 students slept on the Chapel Quad, food services and housekeeping employees went on strike, and most students boycotted the dining halls in support of the employees.*

1960s

ALLEN BUILDING TAKEOVER
February 13, 1969

"We seized the building because we have been negotiating with the Duke administration and faculty for two and a half years. We have no meaningful results. We have exhausted all the so-called proper channels."

—Afro-American Society's statement regarding the takeover

Black students took over the **Allen Building** in an attempt to get the administration to take their demands seriously. They were prepared to barricade themselves within the building for an extended period of time if necessary, but at the promise of negotiations, they agreed to leave. However, dozens of police waiting outside clashed with students on the quad, used tear gas and clubs on the crowds, and arrested students. The protest and its aftermath became a pivotal moment in Duke's history.

Students talk with **President Knight** after the Allen Building takeover.

Prior to the takeover in 1969, students had communicated their demands in other ways, including this **Study-in** held in 1967.

VOICES

Brenda Armstrong M.D.'70 cofounded the **Afro-American Society** at Duke and was its president during the Allen Building takeover in 1969. She became a professor of pediatrics in the division of pediatric cardiology at Duke. She also held the position of associate dean for admissions for Duke's School of Medicine for more than 20 years and was influential in the creation of admissions policies and processes that have helped diversify the medical school student population. Brenda Armstrong passed away in 2018. In 2019, she was honored posthumously with the University Medal, Duke's highest honor.

In 2013, Armstrong was interviewed by **Duke Magazine**: "The takeover of the Allen Building [in February 1969] was a remarkable moment for all of us. Taking up this cause and stepping out [in] faith made us different people. It was so transformative. We had no idea at the time how important it would be, but we left that building with the sense that Duke would be different. We just didn't know how it would be different, and we were still frightened, because we didn't know what the repercussions would be for us." ■

DOUGLAS M. KNIGHT

Douglas M. Knight served as **Duke's president from 1963 to 1969**. *Born in Cambridge, Massachusetts, Knight earned his A.B., M.A., and Ph.D. degrees in English from Yale University. He taught at Yale and was president of Lawrence University in Appleton, Wisconsin, before being named president of Duke in 1963. A poet and a scholar, Knight launched a number of impressive initiatives during his six years as Duke's president. He established the joint M.D.-J.D. and M.D.-Ph.D. degrees and launched the business school and the programs in biomedical engineering and forestry management. Knight also oversaw the addition of the Phytotron and a hyperbaric chamber, the construction of a major wing for Perkins Library, and the establishment of the Duke Art Museum on East Campus.*

In a 2003 memoir, Knight reflected on the struggles he encountered during the '60s and "how the forces that shaped the national debate manifested themselves during his tenure at Duke."

"My whole training and experience to this point had been based in a concept of the university and of liberal education totally grounded in mediation, critical discourse, civility, and the restraint of uncontrolled dogmatism. Now I found that I was required to set all this aside. As a result, I spent—overspent—my energy where I did not want to put it, and so the action of the late sixties was for me a divided action. I was pulled between what I knew the university needed over the decades and what the times demanded immediately." ■

1970s | A DECADE in RETROSPECT

70

Black Studies program *created*

Terry Sanford *becomes Duke's sixth president*

Vietnam Moratorium *demonstration*

Charles Johnson, *M.D., becomes Duke's first Black physician*

Raymond Gavins, *Ph.D., becomes the first Black history professor at Duke*

71

Institute of Policy Sciences and Public Affairs *established, later named for President Terry Sanford*

Duke Comprehensive Cancer Center *established*

Women's varsity athletics *program begins*

72

▸ *Duke's indoor stadium is named for retiring Director of Athletics* Eddie Cameron

Construction begins for **Central Campus**

Duke's first LGBTQIA+ group, the Duke Gay Alliance, is formed

Jean Gaillard Spaulding, *M.D., becomes the first Black woman to graduate from the School of Medicine*

William E. King '61, A.M. '63, Ph.D. '70 *becomes the first university archivist; he would serve in that role for 30 years*

The Woman's College ▸ *merges with Trinity College*

Sanford creates Young Trustee *position*

73

▲ **Duke Eye Center** *opens*

74

Omega Psi Phi *is the first Black fraternity established at Duke*

C. E. Boulware, *Ed.D., becomes Duke's first Black trustee*

76

▲ Michael Holyfield '79 *becomes the first Black student chosen as the Blue Devil mascot*

▲ **Reginaldo "Reggie" Howard** *becomes the first Black student elected as student government president. Tragically, Howard was killed in a car crash before the official start of the term. The Reginaldo Howard Memorial Scholarship is named in his honor.*

Merger invites social and academic changes

Editor's note: The following is the first of two stories examining the proposed merger of Duke's men and women liberal arts colleges.

By Bruce Jabloniski
Staff Writer

The proposed merger of the Woman's College and Trinity College, which from all indications the Board of Trustees will approve in March, will have many undetermined effects upon the undergraduate colleges.

More efficient administrative procedures, more effective representation of undergraduate education concerns and changes in social regulations and admissions policy will be the major results of the merged college.

The merger is the logical next step in the erosion of the co-ordinate college system at Duke. Juanita Kreps, dean of Woman's College, cited the one student government (ASDU) for the two colleges and the fact that men and women live on both campuses as two steps in the "gradual change in the degree of separateness between the two colleges. The only thing that is left is the seperate staffs."

News Analysis

The University has been moving toward a merged college over the years. The breakdown of the ...

filling the merged positions.

It appears that the Undergraduate College of Arts and Sciences will have a greater voice in academic affairs due to a centralized structure. The new dean will represent the undergraduate colleges, as a university administrator, in determining University policy.

Power
Professor William Cartwright of the education department pointed out that the new dean will have more power. Price echoed Cartwright's sentiments and added that the main reason for the merger was to improve the organization of undergraduate academic affairs.

Five women leaders at Duke, 1976. *Left to right: Denise Creech, Duke Union president; Mary Mard, chair of Freewater Films; Lynn Harmonay, chair of the Duke Union Program Council; Goldie Evans, the Duke Union's bookkeeper; and Barbara Hall, Duke Union president.*

▶

77

Jazz musician **Mary Lou Williams** *becomes Artist-in-Residence at Duke*

78

American Dance Festival *relocates to Durham with the help of Duke University*

◀ *The* **Omega Zeta** *chapter of* **Omega Psi Phi Fraternity, Inc.**, *was chartered on April 12, 1974—the first Black Greek organization at Duke. Members of the fraternity perform in front of Duke Chapel in 1974.*

70s

Student pranks *in the 1970s.*

Following the tumult of the late 1960s on campus and nationally, Duke needed a president who could calm campus tensions and provide new leadership. Duke found that leader in **Terry Sanford**, a former governor of North Carolina.

As governor, Sanford focused on strengthening education, combating poverty, and expanding civil rights. Under his leadership as governor, state funding for public schools nearly doubled. He took the position—rare in the South at the time—of supporting integration and working to undo segregation. He was instrumental in making the Research Triangle Park a hub of research and industry. A 1990 Harvard University study would rank Sanford as one of the nation's 10 best governors in the 20th century.

In 1970, Sanford began his 15-year tenure as president of Duke University. A gifted politician, he was comfortable engaging with student protestors and often invited them into his office to sit down and talk with him. While he was Duke's president, he also ran—twice—for president of the United States. Because of his political background, Sanford recognized the need for a university to engage with the world, so he founded the Institute for Policy Sciences and Public Affairs. The interdisciplinary program to train future public leaders was among the first in the nation; it would later be named the Sanford School of Public Policy in his honor.

The 1970s also saw investments in other key academic programs. In

During Orientation Week, students wave from **Alspaugh Residence Hall** *on East Campus.*

1971, the computer science program began; it would become a department in 1973. The Biomedical Engineering (BME) division became a department in 1971. The following year, Duke became the first college in the U.S. to have an accredited undergraduate major in BME.

In response to the protests of the 1960s, many at Duke worked to reduce social inequalities on campus. In 1972, the incoming freshman class included 82 Black students—more than twice as many as ever before. The Black Studies program had been established in 1969, and faculty and students worked to gain recognition and funding for the program. Today, the Department of African & African American Studies continues to offer Duke students interdisciplinary teaching and scholarship on Africa and people of African descent around the world.

The 1970s also brought changes for women at Duke. In 1972, the Woman's College and Trinity College merged into the Trinity College of Arts and Sciences. The merger allowed greater latitude for men to live on East Campus and women on West Campus. Under the Woman's College, women students had been subject to stricter disciplinary standards, and many students chafed at the double standard in how men and women students were treated. Not everyone agreed with the merger, however: some students and faculty maintained that women students would be better served by continuing to have their own deans, mentors, and student government.

William Shingleton, *M.D., was a distinguished surgeon at Duke and founding director of the Duke Comprehensive Cancer Center. Under his leadership, Duke became recognized nationally as a leader in cancer research and care.*

While Duke women had long participated in intramurals and majored in health and physical education, in 1971 Duke started its women's varsity athletics program. The move came in advance of the passage of Title IX in 1972, which prohibited discrimination on the basis of sex. One of eight varsity women's sports introduced in the 1970s, the volleyball team generated campus excitement in 1976 by posting a 36–6 record and reaching the national tournament.

These strategic investments in interdisciplinary teaching and research, as well as moves toward greater inclusivity, all contributed toward Duke's rise from a Southern university with a strong regional reputation to one of national prominence. ∎

CANCER CARE *at* DUKE

In 1973, Duke was named a **Comprehensive Cancer Center** *by the National Cancer Institute (NCI), becoming one of the nation's original eight such centers. William Shingleton, one of the signers of the National Cancer Act of 1971, was appointed the inaugural cancer center director by William G. Anlyan, vice president for health affairs.*

In 1975, the Edwin L. Jones Cancer Research Building opened, and three years later, the Edwin A. Morris Building opened, bringing together inpatient and outpatient cancer care while providing space to pursue the concept of multidisciplinary care.

In 1977, the Citizens Advisory Council was created, which later became the DCI Board of Advisors. This long-standing group of volunteers focuses on education, advocacy, and support for the center's mission.

In 2024, the Duke Cancer Institute is one of the premier cancer centers in the United States. As an NCI-designated comprehensive cancer center, the Duke Cancer Institute has a level of cancer expertise only found in the top 4 percent of U.S. centers. The Duke Cancer Center, which opened in 2012, is a state-of-the-art patient care facility devoted solely to providing high-quality outpatient cancer care services.

1970s

President **Terry Sanford** greets Duke employees.

"This Kind of University" | *Excerpt from Inaugural Address of President Terry Sanford, October 18, 1970*

"But the full story of Duke University does not lead through the names of presidents and benefactors alone. It spreads across and includes sacrifice, achieving, suffering, giving, the lifetime devotions of the thousands of scholars and teachers who defined Duke University and infused it with life and personality by their service, scholarship, and intellect. It includes the tens of thousands of students who went from here to prove the worth of Alma Mater, and unsung donors by the thousands whose gifts make up the sinew of the body. . . . It is not enough for Duke University to aspire to be the best—the best of what? Rather it is for Duke University to be unique, with its own talents and strengths, in its own setting, with its own history and heritage. I do not propose that we seek for ourselves a homogenized pattern of the half-dozen great private universities of the nation of which we are one, or that we try to 'catch up' or follow any university, no matter what its prestigious position. Simply to do as some other university does, to teach as it teaches, to operate as it operates, to accept it as our model, would make our best success but a carbon copy. We strive to be Duke University, an institution seeking the highest scholarly attainment, and using to the fullest its own peculiar resources and creative capabilities." ∎

1970s

BLACK STUDIES *at* DUKE

The Black Studies program was established in 1969. **Mark Anthony Neal**, Ph.D., the James B. Duke Professor of African & African American Studies and chair of the department, commented in 2020 on the fiftieth anniversary of the program:

"Institutions face tremendous scrutiny and censure when they fail to embrace diversity. From the vantage point of being among the many departments in the Trinity College of Arts and Sciences committed to preparing students for the world beyond Duke's campus—where there is a continuous need for diverse perspectives and people—Black Studies helps prepare students for that world.

Graduates of our department have been able to apply their training with us to work in the fields of medicine, public policy, and law and criminal justice, to name just a few examples. And as the continent of Africa emerges as a collaborative partner for so many global entities, of course there will be a need for journalists, anthropologists, and historians trained in contemporary Africa.

As one of the leading Black studies units in the country, and one that epitomizes the interdisciplinary spirit of Duke—we boast economists, historians, literary theorists, art historians, a choreographer, political scientists, journalists, digital humanists, cultural theorists, social scientists, and a geneticist among our faculty. African & African American Studies is well-positioned to continue its impact in the field and beyond." ∎

Suzanne "Dean Sue" Wasiolek
'76, M.H.A.'78, L.L.M.'93 had a 40-year career in Student Affairs, serving as dean of students and later as faculty-in-residence in Gilbert-Addoms Residence Hall on East Campus.

Raymond (Ray) Gavins, *Ph.D., joined the Duke faculty in 1970. He was the first Black person hired by the history department and one of the first faculty to teach courses in Duke's Black Studies program. A scholar of African American and American history, Gavins helped launch the department's oral history program and the Behind the Veil Project of the Center for Documentary Studies, which conducted more than 1,350 interviews with Black Americans to document life during the Jim Crow era. Over his 45 years at Duke, Gavins was also a beloved teacher, and many of his former graduate students are now historians at colleges and universities across America.*

Professor **Paul Kramer**, Ph.D., talks with School of Forestry graduate student **Patrick Tesha** M.F.'70 in the Phytotron, ca. March 1970.

A class with the Rev. **Joseph B. Bethea**, who was the founding director of the Office of Black Church Studies from 1972 to 1977 and went on to become a bishop in the United Methodist Church.

President Sanford saw that the burgeoning new field of public policy studies could bring the best of academia to inform practical solutions in the real world. Through public policy, the strengths of the traditional social sciences—economics, political science, and other disciplines—could help offer policy solutions. Sanford convinced **Joel Fleishman** (inset) who had served as Sanford's legal aide during his gubernatorial term and was then part of Yale's Institute of Social Science, to come to Duke to design a new program and run it.

Founded in 1971 as the **Institute of Policy Sciences and Public Affairs** and led by Fleishman, Duke's program quickly distinguished itself by emphasizing undergraduate education and incorporating perspectives from the humanities.

Bruce Kuniholm was hired at the Institute after graduating with his Ph.D. in 1976. He served as director of undergraduate studies and subsequently as one of its most influential directors. **The Sanford Institute** became Duke's tenth school in 2009, when it was renamed the Sanford School of Public Policy, and Kuniholm served as its first dean from 2009 to 2013.

Fifty years after Duke embraced public policy, the Sanford School's M.P.P. program is ranked by U.S. News & World Report as a top program in environmental policy, public policy analysis, social policy, and health policy. It continues to attract joint-degree students from many of Duke's other schools. ■

Public policy students meet with **Bonnie Bain** in her office. Bain was hired in 1972 as the first director of internship programs.

1970s

WOMEN'S ATHLETICS *at* DUKE

In 1971, in advance of the passage of **Title IX**, Duke started its varsity intercollegiate athletics program for women. At the same time, Duke became a charter member of the Association of Intercollegiate Athletics for Women (AIAW), an organization that at its peak included 1,000 schools. Duke competed in the AIAW until the NCAA began to include women's sports in the early '80s.

Volleyball was one of eight varsity women's sports established during the 1970s, playing its first official season in 1971. The 1976 Blue Devils were Duke's first great women's team, posting a 36–6 record and reaching the AIAW national tournament in Austin, Texas. **Leslie C. Lewis** '79, who served as a team captain, was Duke's first scholarship volleyball player and one of the first five female student-athletes to receive an athletic scholarship at Duke. In 2021–22, marking 50 years of Duke women's athletics, Lewis recalled, "What was really fun was moving

out of the gym on East Campus and moving over to Cameron to get to play our games in Cameron Indoor Stadium. That was wonderful and exciting to play on that great floor."

In 2024, Duke University sponsors 13 women's athletic programs in basketball, soccer, softball, volleyball, rowing, track & field, cross country, tennis, lacrosse, golf, fencing, field hockey, and swimming & diving. These programs have collectively won 8 team national championships, 12 individual national titles, and 64 ACC championships and have produced several Olympic medalists. Most recently, softball became the latest women's sports program added to the Blue Devil family, with its first season of competition taking place in 2018. ■

(Clockwise from top left)
Tara McCarthy '81, a 5'7" guard, was the first scholarship player on the **Duke women's basketball team**.

Duke had a **varsity women's gymnastics** team in the 1970s. The program was cut in 1984 when women's programs were added in indoor and outdoor track and cross country.

Pat Jensen '80 was a member of the **Duke volleyball squad** from 1976 to 1979.

Duke **field hockey**, October 1974.

In 1977–78, **Ellison Goodall '78** earned track and cross country All-America honors and won the AAU national championship in the 10,000 meters. Because Duke did not have a women's varsity program at the time, Goodall often trained with the men's team. The program began varsity competition in 1984.

MENTOR

AL BUEHLER

*Al Buehler, Duke's longtime **head coach of men's cross country and track & field,** joined the Blue Devils in 1955. During his 45-year tenure at Duke, Buehler coached ten All-American athletes, seven Penn Relay champions, six ACC championship cross country teams, and five Olympians. In 1972, 1984, and 1988, Buehler served as team manager for the U.S. Olympic Track & Field Teams in Munich, Los Angeles, and Seoul, respectively.*

Buehler gained additional fame in the 1970s as a track meet organizer and official. In 1970, Buehler was elected president of the NCAA Track and Field Coaches Association and directed the first annual U.S. Olympic summer training camp at Wallace Wade Stadium. Buehler worked with North Carolina Central University's track coach and interim chancellor, Leroy T. Walker, to plan the Pan Africa–USA International Track Meet, which was hosted by Duke in 1971.

When he retired in 2000, following the NCAA Track and Field Championships in Durham, the beloved three-mile path in Duke Forest that loops around the golf course was named the Al Buehler Trail in his honor.

NEW SPACES

Mary Duke Biddle Music Building *under construction.*

*President Terry Sanford listens to Mary Duke Biddle Trent Semans, granddaughter of Benjamin N. Duke, at the dedication of the **Mary Duke Biddle Music Building** in 1974. The building was named for Semans's mother.*

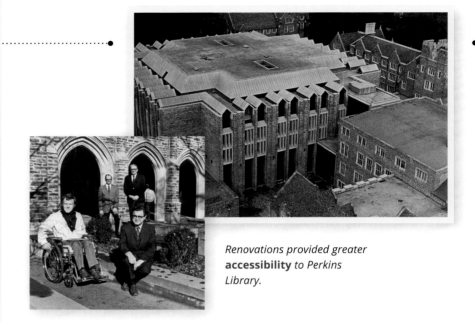

Renovations provided greater **accessibility** *to Perkins Library.*

The **Central Campus Apartments** *were constructed between 1972 and 1975 as housing for graduate students and students with families.*

1970s

Site of the Future
UNIVERSITY
CENTER

Sign Erected By Phi Delta Theta Fraternity

Impatient students express their frustration with the slow pace of plans for the new university center. The groundbreaking finally began in 1979 for what would become the **Bryan Center**.

Saturday, December 11, 1976   PAGE 3

University Center Begins

Groundbreaking was held for the new $8 million University Center yesterday at Duke University. The new center will be located behind Page Auditorium. It will house most students activities and will provide a home for theater at Duke, an art gallery, a restaurant and the university stores. Shown at ground-breaking exercises yesterday are, left to right, John Alexander McMahon, chairman of the board of trustees at Duke; Terry Sanford, president of the university; Juke Phelps, executive director of the Duke Student Union; and Jeff Garland, head of the Student Project for University Development.

—Sun Staff Photo By Thornton

Officials Attend Groundbreaking
For New Duke 'University Center'

By CARL BOSWELL

Ceremonies to kick off construction of a new University Center at Duke University were held yesterday behind Page Auditorium, site of the new building.

It will be located just northwest of Flowers Building on West Campus, within walking distance of the central, law, and science estimated at $8 million.

According to Jake Phelps, director of the University Union, which will coordinate activities in the center, Duke has received gifts and pledges of more than $3.9 million for construction costs of the center, including a number of major gifts from foundations and corporations.

Seniors in the classes of 1975 rooms and office space.

R. J. Reynolds Industries has already made a major gift to the center to fund construction of the performing arts theater, and the Emma Sheafer Foundation has funded construction of the laboratory theater. The theater complex is expected to be in use by 1978.

Facilities will also be made available for arts and crafts, past, groups such as the student paper, student government and special interest groups, have been scattered around the campus so people with similar interests have had little chance to work together. In the new center, there will be space for these groups to work together.

Other facilities will include a large multi-purpose room which will be capable...

1 9 7 0 s

1980s | A DECADE in RETROSPECT

80

▲

Mike Krzyzewski *hired as men's basketball head coach*

New Duke University Hospital opens

Duke cultural anthropologist Ernestine Friedl, Ph.D., becomes the first woman to serve as dean of Trinity College of Arts and Sciences

81

Nixon Presidential Library *controversially proposed to be located at Duke*

82

Paul Farmer, *M.D., Ph.D., a global health pioneer and Trustee Emeritus, graduates*

83

Mary Lou Williams Center for Black Culture *opens*

Women's Studies program *established*

Historian John Hope Franklin, *Ph.D., hired*

WXDU *begins broadcasting*

▼

85

First AZT clinical trials conducted at Duke

H. Keith H. Brodie, *M.D., named Duke's seventh president*

86

The tent village before the Duke-UNC game is named "Krzyzewskiville"

Men's soccer wins *Duke's first-ever team national championship*

▼

88

▲

President Ronald Reagan *visits Duke on February 8, 1988, to speak at a forum on substance abuse in the workplace*

WXDU takes to the airwaves

By JOE McHUGH

Mike Schoenfeld, WXDU's programming director

★ EXTRA! ★ ★ READ ALL ABOUT IT! ★ ★ EXTRA! ★

THE CHRONICLE

DUKE UNIVERSITY · DURHAM, NORTH CAROLINA   CIRCULATION: 15,000   VOL. 82, NO. 72

MONDAY, DECEMBER 15, 1986

DUKE WON, AKRON ZIP

NCAA title is school's first ever

By MICHAEL LEBER

TACOMA, Wash. — The view is pretty nice when you are on top of the world. Ask any player or coach on the Duke soccer team and he will tell you.

Do the dome: Team members celebrate after 1-0 victory in championship game Saturday in Tacoma.

JANE PISACENEYA/THE CHRONICLE

HOT COLLEGES
And How They Get That Way
BY MICHAEL WINERIP

The cover story of the *New York Times Magazine* on November 18, 1984, read HOT COLLEGES. The photo was unmistakably Duke—smiling students, Duke sweatshirt, Chapel in the background—and Duke was unmistakably a Hot College.

But how, as the article asked, did Duke "get that way"?

The Bryan University Center *opened in 1982, named for Joseph M. and Kathleen Bryan. Home to the Rathskeller ("the Rat"), the Boyd-Pishko Café ("the B-P"), and the popular video game arcade The Devil's Quarters—as well as two theaters, the campus bookstore, and a post office—the Bryan Center became a hub of campus life.*

80s

Cameron Crazies *chant during the Duke men's basketball game against UNC in 1989.*

By the 1980s, President Terry Sanford's outrageous ambition had led to key investments that were paying off with increased visibility. In 1983, Sanford hired **Phillip Griffiths**, Ph.D., a Harvard mathematician, to be Duke's provost. Despite having no administrative experience, Griffiths proved to be a quick study, meeting with faculty across the university, asking about their challenges, and building up Duke's academic excellence and reputation, especially in the humanities.

At the same time, Duke University Medical Center was expanding and becoming known for outstanding clinical care. The new $94.5-million, 616-bed Duke University Hospital opened in 1980, bringing Duke's total number of patient beds to over 1,000.

In 1983 and 1984, Duke staff and faculty showed courage and compassion on the front lines of the emerging HIV/AIDS epidemic, working to understand the new epidemic and meet the needs of patients who were facing stigma and discrimination. Duke quickly became a national leader in HIV/AIDS research and was one of two hospitals to conduct the first human clinical trials of AZT.

Duke gained a new opportunity to leverage the strength of the medical center when **H. Keith H. Brodie**, a distinguished psychiatrist, succeeded Sanford as Duke's seventh president in 1985. Brodie knew that having the School of Medicine, the hospital, and the university co-located on one campus gave Duke a distinctive advantage for collaboration. As chancellor and then as president, Brodie worked to create joint research and teaching and service programs.

And of course, no one can underestimate the impact of the arrival in 1980 of a young coach hired to lead Duke's men's basketball program. Introduced at a press conference, **Mike Krzyzewski** had to begin by spelling and pronouncing his name. Asked if he was surprised to be offered the position, he replied with confidence, "I had a gut feeling that I would get the job. . . . I felt that Duke was right for me, and I hope I'm right for Duke."

The 1980s saw an explosion of college basketball on television, fueled in part by the launch of ESPN in 1979 and the expansion of the NCAA tournament to 64 teams in 1985, and Duke and Coach K rode the wave of popularity. With their faces painted blue and a new nickname, the "Cameron Crazies" and their famously intimidating cheers and taunts captured television audiences. Students also began to set up tents in order to gain entry to the Duke-UNC game, starting a Duke tradition they called Krzyzewskiville, or Kville, in honor of Duke's coach. And the fans were rewarded: Coach K took his team to the championship game in 1986 and made additional trips to the Final Four in 1988, 1989, and 1990, a run of success that would eventually lead to 13 career Final Fours—the most of any coach.

The cumulative effect of this national exposure created an image of Duke as a place that took its academics seriously and also knew how to have fun—a place bursting with creativity and energy and school spirit. This hot college was well on its way. ∎

VOICES

This essay appeared in the Duke yearbook, **The Chanticleer,** *in 1987.*

"*In drama classes at Duke,* students learn that the play doesn't begin until something comes along to change the status quo; that is, an intrusion explodes the status of the world on stage, so that the main elements of the world will never be the same again.

I would hope that as you look back on your education at Duke, you find it to have been an intrusion into your life at a critical moment in your development; that the equilibrium you had established in relationships with your family and friends at home, in your educational experience in high school, in church and civic activities—that this equilibrium was exploded, re-established, and exploded again as your collision with ideas and knowledge pushed you into new growth and sensitivity. A liberal arts education should be an intrusion; it should change your world forever by changing the way you see and experience it.

A good playwright knows that an audience needs to be able to compare two worlds on the stage—the world at rest and the world interrupted by something new and, for a time, unexplained. And what the audience must tolerate is suspense, a state of unease and tension, even discomfort, at not knowing.

A good education in the arts and sciences is like this; it should confront and explode your preconceptions; it should challenge and broaden your point of view, placing you for a time inside other people, other cultures, other times, to compare yourself, and to grow. Most of all, it should make you uncomfortable with not knowing, uneasy about complacency, and tolerant of the lack of closure that defines the human condition."

H. Keith H. Brodie
Duke University President, 1985–93

H. Keith H. Brodie *was inaugurated on September 29, 1985, as Duke's seventh president. Previously professor and chairman of the Department of Psychiatry in the Duke School of Medicine and director of psychiatric services at Duke University Medical Center, Brodie had served as chancellor since 1982.*

HUMANITIES

During the late 1980s, the **Duke English Department** *rose to national prominence. Its charismatic chair,* **Stanley Fish,** *Ph.D., recruited star faculty who made the department a vanguard in literary studies—and a target in the "culture wars" of the 1980s. Fish also served as the co-director of Duke University Press.*

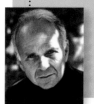

Wallace Fowlie, *Ph.D., has been called "America's most celebrated professor of French." His translation of poems by the 19th-century French poet Arthur Rimbaud was studied and memorized by rock stars Jim Morrison and Patti Smith. In the eighties, Professor Fowlie was a rock star on Duke's campus, with his classes so popular that many students could not secure one of the sought-after spots.*

1980s

A renowned pianist, composer, teacher, and humanitarian, **Mary Lou Williams**—known as "the first lady of the piano"—performed with numerous jazz legends and taught at Duke as an Artist-in-Residence from 1977 until her death in 1981. The Mary Lou Williams Center for Black Culture was established at Duke in 1983 and named in her honor.

Staff of the Mary Lou Williams Center for Black Culture: Edward Hill, Ph.D., the first director of the center, is standing second from the right. Through lectures, performances, exhibits, and informal gatherings, the Mary Lou Williams Center continues to be a welcoming and dynamic campus space celebrating Black culture.

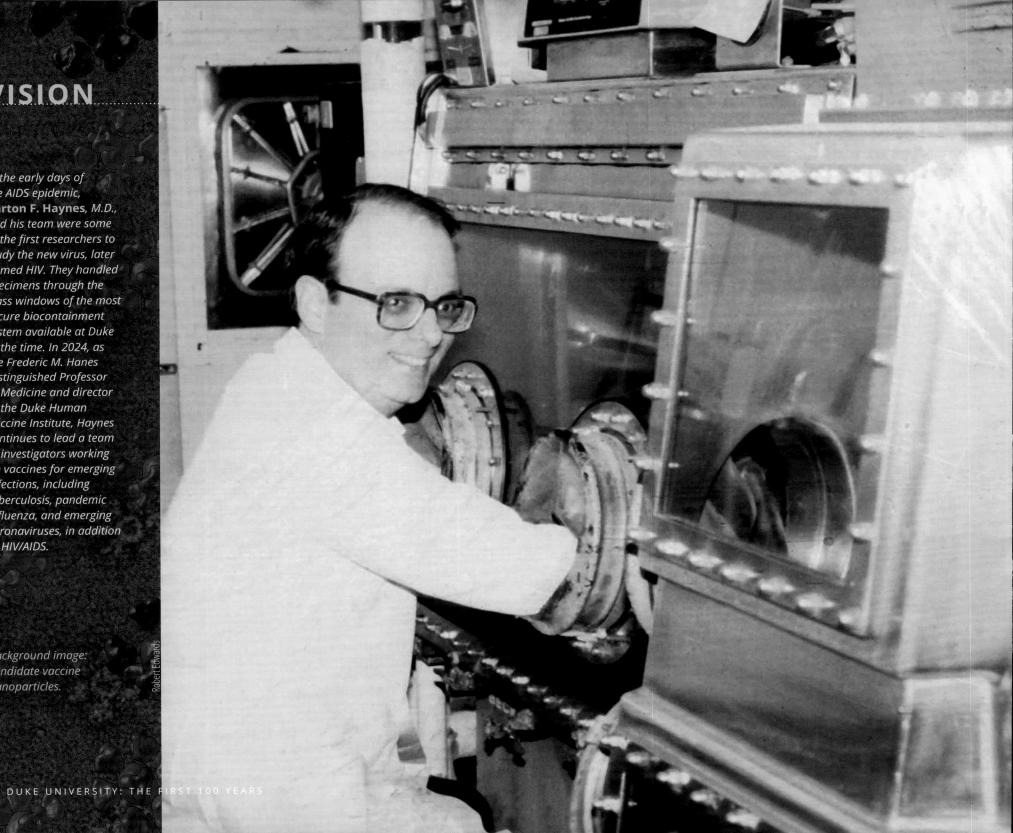

VISION

In the early days of the AIDS epidemic, **Barton F. Haynes,** *M.D., and his team were some of the first researchers to study the new virus, later named HIV. They handled specimens through the glass windows of the most secure biocontainment system available at Duke at the time. In 2024, as the Frederic M. Hanes Distinguished Professor of Medicine and director of the Duke Human Vaccine Institute, Haynes continues to lead a team of investigators working on vaccines for emerging infections, including tuberculosis, pandemic influenza, and emerging coronaviruses, in addition to HIV/AIDS.*

Background image: candidate vaccine nanoparticles.

Robert Edwards

1980s

The new 616-bed **Duke University Hospital** *opened in 1980, north of the original hospital, and is known as Duke North.*

COACH

On March 18, 1980, Mike Krzyzewski was named head coach of Duke men's basketball. The 33-year-old West Point graduate had been the head coach at his alma mater for the previous five years. After a rocky start at Duke, his 1982 recruiting class turned the program around and went to the NCAA championship game in 1986. Their story was featured in a documentary called The Class That Saved Coach K.

Coach K addresses his team in the Duke locker room in 1983.

WINNERS NEVER GIVE UP

1980s

When the chants and taunts in Cameron Indoor Stadium were getting too rowdy and profane, Duke President Terry Sanford calmed the crowd with his famous "Avuncular Letter," urging students to be "clever but clean, devastating but decent," and signed it **"Uncle Terry."**

The first Krzyzewskiville: *In March 1986, a group of students from Mirecourt Dorm pitched tents outside Cameron Indoor Stadium in order to guarantee spots at the Duke-UNC game. By game time, 75 tents were up. The tent village got a new name—Krzyzewskiville—and a new Duke tradition was born. (Duke beat UNC, 82–74.)*

Duke University
Durham
North Carolina 27706

Office of the President   January 17, 1984

AN AVUNCULAR LETTER

To My Duke Students:

The enthusiasm of Duke students in Cameron Indoor Stadium during basketball games is legendary, especially at ACC games. That's great! It is as if we had a sixth man (maybe seventh, eighth, or tenth sometimes) playing on the floor.

But hold a minute--I have a reservation about all that. There is a recognizable line between enthusiasm and cheapness.

It is generally assumed that a person resorting in conversation to profanity and obscenities is short of an adequate vocabulary. That is doubly true in public utterances.

Resorting to the use of obscenities in cheers and chants at ball games indicates a lack of vocabulary, a lack of cleverness, a lack of ideas, a lack of class, and a lack of respect for other people. We are, I am sorry to report, gaining an unequaled reputation as a student body that doesn't have a touch of class.

I don't think we need to be crude and obscene to be effectively enthusiastic. We can cheer and taunt with style; that should be the Duke trademark. Crudeness, profanity, and cheapness should not be our reputation--but it is.

I suggest that we change. Talk this matter over in your various residential houses. Think of something clever but clean, devastating but decent, mean but wholesome, witty and forceful but G-rated for television, and try it at the next game.

We have too much going for us as an outstanding university to tolerate the reputation we now have for being so crude and inarticulate that we must resort to profanity and obscenities at ball games.

I hope you will discipline yourselves and your fellow students. This request is in keeping with my commitment to self-government for students. It should not be up to me to enforce proper behavior that signifies the intelligence of Duke students. You should do it. Reprove those who make us all look bad. Shape up your own language.

I hate for us to have the reputation of being stupid.

With best wishes,

Uncle Terry

President Terry Sanford

LE TERRY, THE DEVIL MADE US DO IT

HEY MATT DOHERTY, "Ever try ___?"

A HEARTY WELCOME TO DEAN SMITH

1980s

As many did on college campuses in the 1980s, **Duke students advocated for reproductive rights** *and organized Take Back the Night marches to raise awareness about sexual assault.*

At **freshman orientation**, incoming students were given their class directories and ushered into a community that offered on-campus fun and opportunities to engage with the world.

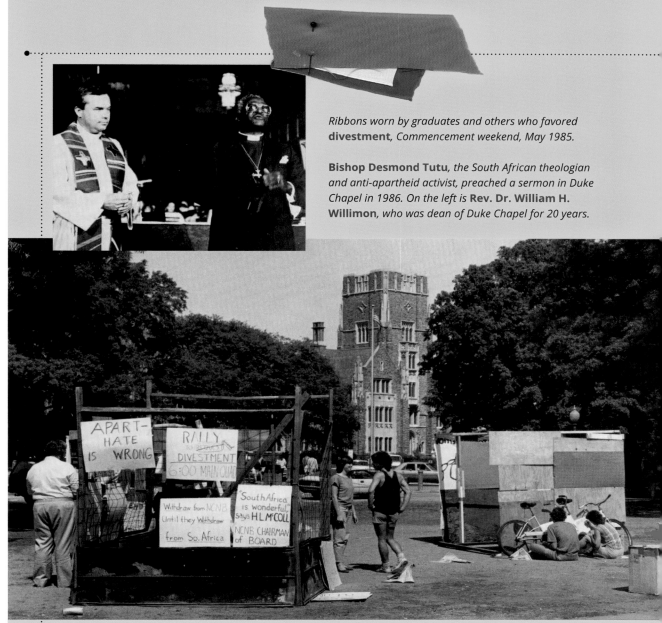

Ribbons worn by graduates and others who favored **divestment**, *Commencement weekend, May 1985.*

Bishop Desmond Tutu, *the South African theologian and anti-apartheid activist, preached a sermon in Duke Chapel in 1986. On the left is* **Rev. Dr. William H. Willimon,** *who was dean of Duke Chapel for 20 years.*

The 1980s saw widespread protests on American college campuses regarding **divestment** *from companies conducting business in South Africa. In 1986, along with hundreds of universities across the country, the Duke University Board of Trustees voted to divest. The international pressure helped to bring about the collapse of the racist South African regime.*

1980s

THE ERA

The 1980s at Duke literally **rocked**.

These are just some of the performances that took place on campus from 1980 through 1989. Many of these artists were at the height of their careers when they took to the stage at Springfest, in Page Auditorium, or in Cameron Indoor Stadium.

R.E.M.
September 25

Billy Idol
September 6

The Psychedelic Furs
October 10

Cyndi Lauper *with*
The Bangles
November 2

John Prine
March 5

The Go-Go's *with*
A Flock of Seagulls
September 15

80

81

82

83

84

Jimmy Buffett
February 22

David Crosby
April 23

Peter Tosh
July 31

The Beach Boys
October 25

**The Grateful
Dead**
September 23

R.E.M. *with*
**The English
Beat**
March 26

Pousette-Dart Band
April 9

The Cars
November 22

Psychedelic Furs
January 20

Eric Clapton
April 18

UB40
October 16

THE CHRO

MONDAY, OCTOBER 5, 1987 · ○   DUKE UNIVERSITY   DURHAM, NORTH CAROLINA

Attacks
steps; sus

By ROCKY ROSEN

Wearing his harborcoat, R.E.M.'s Michael Stipe croons to a crowd of eager
fans.

R.E.M. 'documents' return

Georgia band fills Cameron with fine worksongs

Air Force

Bruce Hornsby
September 30

**Echo and the
Bunnymen**
February 20

The Cure
September 20

85   **86**   **87**   **88**   **89**

Paul Young
November 5

Elvis Costello/Branford Marsalis
October 10

Elvis Costello *with* **Nick Lowe**
April 21

R.E.M. *with* **10,000 Maniacs**
October 3

Love and Rockets *with*
Jane's Addiction
November 16

UB40
October 4

**Fine Young
Cannibals**
September 27

Bob Dylan
November 8

Blues Traveler
December 2

1990s | A DECADE *in* RETROSPECT

90

Center for Documentary Studies *opens*

91

Men's basketball wins back-to-back national championships

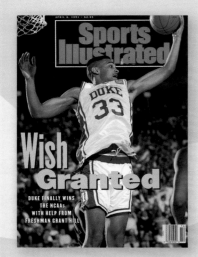

Sports Illustrated *and the* Chronicle *celebrated Duke's* **national championship** *win in 1991.*

92

Mi Gente, Duke's Latinx student association, is formed

93

Nannerl O. Keohane, *Ph.D., becomes Duke's eighth president*

Duke Student Government *replaces ASDU (Associated Students of Duke University)*

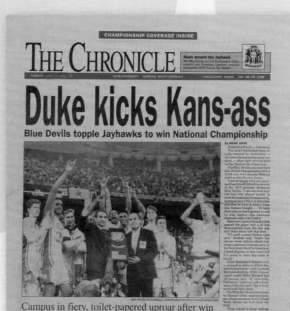

THE CHRONICLE
Duke kicks Kans-ass
Blue Devils topple Jayhawks to win National Championship

Campus in fiery, toilet-papered uproar after win

94

Levine Science Research Center *(LSRC) opens, designed to support interdisciplinary research*

95

The School of the Environment *is renamed the Nicholas School of the Environment in recognition of a $20 million gift by trustee Peter M. Nicholas '64*

Kenan Institute for Ethics *is established*

East Campus *becomes the home for all first-year students at Duke*

96

Center for LGBT Life is created, later renamed the Center for Sexual and Gender Diversity

Bass Society of Fellows *created with a gift from Anne T. and Robert Bass to recognize faculty who excel in both research and teaching*

Duke celebrates its **75th anniversary** in 1999 with fireworks over the Chapel.

97

▲

Former president Jimmy Carter is Duke's commencement speaker

Led by Duke junior Tico Almeida '99, the group **Students Against Sweatshops** *pushes for the adoption of standards for the manufacture of Duke apparel*
▼

98

▲

Former president **George H. W. Bush** *is Duke's commencement speaker*

Vanessa Webb *becomes Duke's first individual NCAA champion in women's singles tennis*

The Campaign for Duke *is launched; it would raise more than $2 billion*

99

Kristina M. Johnson, Ph.D., becomes dean of engineering, the first woman to hold that role

In recognition of a gift from trustee emeritus Edmund T. Pratt Jr. B.S.E.E.'47, the school is named the Pratt School of Engineering

Freeman Center for Jewish Life *opens*

Women's golf team wins its first national championship

Duke celebrates its 75th anniversary

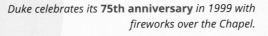

Victory bonfires *on West Campus after big wins for men's basketball became a cherished Duke tradition in the 1990s, as seen in this celebration on Clocktower Quad after Duke defeated Florida in the NCAA semifinal game in 1994.*

19

90s

Duke students *welcome crews from the popular morning television show* Good Morning, America *to campus.*

The back-to-back national championships won by the men's basketball team in 1991 and 1992 were a joyful start to the 1990s. Coach **Mike Krzyzewski** and his team of dazzling talent that included **Christian Laettner '92, Bobby Hurley '93,** and **Grant Hill '94** brought the titles home to Duke in decisive fashion. Thirty years later, the 1992 Eastern Regional final game is considered one of the greatest college basketball games of all time, with Laettner hitting "The Shot" against Kentucky in the final 2.1 seconds of overtime for the win.

As Duke exulted in its new national status, faculty and students began to think about what kind of university it could be.

In his Founders' Day speech in 1992, Duke alumnus and celebrated English professor **Reynolds Price '55** urged the university to foster a more intellectual environment that would "nurture the literal heart of a great university."

Christoph Guttentag had been hired in 1992 to lead Duke's Office of Undergraduate Admissions. With applications rising and acceptance rates falling, Duke was attracting some of the most talented high school students in America. The SAT scores of those applicants were going up, and they were more diverse, too. In 1987, just 15.2 percent of the entering class were students of color; by 1998, that number was 30 percent. At the same time, administrators worked to create a climate where ideas were welcomed, both in and out of the classroom.

This effort found a new champion when **Nannerl Overholser Keohane** became Duke's eighth president in 1993. Nan Keohane was the first woman to serve as president of Duke and one of the first at any major American university. A political theorist, Keohane had previously been president of Wellesley College, her alma mater.

Under Keohane's leadership, internationalization became a strategic priority. Duke faculty pursued international research projects, forged partnerships around the world, and worked to prepare graduates for an increasingly diverse and global economy. In 1996, the Fuqua School of Business welcomed 39 students from 11 countries as the first students in the Global Executive MBA program, or GEMBA. **Rex Adams**, the Fuqua dean, called GEMBA "the most significant innovation in management education in fifty years."

As Keohane wrote in 1998, "Our goal is to become more thoroughly international in our curriculum, our outreach, the people who teach and learn with us, so that being a global institution is not an add-on, but an intrinsic part of everything we do."

Closer to home, Duke was also working to strengthen its relationship with the City of Durham. In 1996, Keohane and **John Burness**, then the vice president for public affairs and government relations, established the Duke-Durham Neighborhood Partnership.

1990s

Working with local residents in 12 Durham neighborhoods and seven public schools, the initiative helped to increase home ownership, improve student achievement, and expand access to health care.

As Duke worked to create a more supportive living and learning community for its increasingly diverse student population, the idea arose to convert East Campus into a residential campus for first-year students. While the proposal was initially controversial, after the first class moved in, it was an immediate success. First-year students loved their new home on East Campus. And Duke continued to expand its sense of welcome and community. ■

*Students relaxing on **Brown Residence Hall bench**, 1994.*

*Since 1995, all first-year students have started their Duke journey on **East Campus**, where they find a welcoming residential community and academic deans and advisors as they begin their college career. Each house on East Campus also has a connected Faculty-in-Residence. Today, through QuadEx, East Campus residence halls are paired and connected to Quads on West Campus. This link between East and West Campus offers continuity of residential communities.*

MENTOR

A Duke alumnus and a Rhodes Scholar, **Reynolds Price** *taught English at Duke for 50 years. An acclaimed poet, novelist, and memoirist, Professor Price used his deep, rich voice to make literature come alive, whether he was reading* Paradise Lost *in the classroom or spooky ghost stories on Halloween in the Gothic Reading Room. The author of acclaimed novels like* A Long and Happy Life *and* Kate Vaiden, *Price also wrote about his experience with disability from the 1980s onward.*

1990s

As president of Duke, Nan Keohane championed increased faculty diversity and promoted the hiring and advancement of women faculty, building on work begun in the 1980s. This 1993 photo shows members of the **faculty of the Duke Divinity School**.

President Keohane with **former presidents** Knight and Sanford at her inauguration, October 23, 1993.

Nannerl ("Nan") Overholser Keohane was inaugurated as Duke's eighth president in 1993. She was the first woman to be named president of Duke and one of a very few women university presidents in America at the time.

"The benefits of belonging to a community dedicated to advancing knowledge should extend to all its members. This means job training and skills development for workers and staff; encouragement to attend lectures or take course credits; challenging assignments and opportunities for personal growth through work. It means respect for the dignity of everyone who contributes to this university. All of us should find in the university a place that expands our understanding of the world and provides us with the tools we need to play our part in the common enterprise."

—**President Nan Keohane**, from her inaugural
address, October 23, 1993

As student body president, **Hardy Vieux '93** (inset) was a vocal advocate for faculty diversity. Vieux also served as president of the Duke Alumni Association from 2010 to 2012.

Two scholars recruited in the early '90s spent their careers at Duke— **Karla Holloway**, Ph.D., James B. Duke Professor of English (above), and **Richard J. Powell**, Ph.D., John Spencer Bassett Professor of Art and Art History (far right).

FACULTY DIVERSITY

1990s

The BLACK FACULTY INITIATIVE

While Duke's recruitment of minority undergraduate and graduate students was gaining strength, the university's efforts to recruit more diverse faculty initially sputtered. The Black Faculty Initiative had passed in 1988. At that time, out of Duke's 1,399 faculty members, just 31 were Black. The Black Faculty Initiative committed Duke to adding one African American faculty member in every Duke hiring unit—from art history to zoology. Despite early momentum, five years later, Duke was nowhere close to fulfilling its goal. Buttons on campus asked the pointed question "Have You Seen Them?"

In 1993, the university took up the effort again. This time, the university reached its new goal of doubling the number of Black faculty members. At the same time, a faculty task force on diversity pushed Duke to think more broadly about fostering a more welcoming community.

"If Duke had not made diversification of its faculty and student body a priority, the university would not be the vibrant and intellectually stimulating and challenging institution that it is today. Diversification of the faculty brought with it new lines of inquiry and areas of research and teaching that were not present before. Moreover, in some instances Duke was able to establish itself as a premier place of study in several areas that did not exist before the push to recruit a more diverse faculty."

—**Paula D. McClain**, *Ph.D., James B. Duke Distinguished Professor of Political Science and Professor of Public Policy, commenting in 2009 on Duke's efforts in the 1990s. Dean of The Graduate School from 2012 to 2022, McClain was the first Black person to be named dean of one of Duke's schools.*

1990s

DUKE & DURHAM

"The Neighborhood Partnership initiative has been one of the best aspects of our outreach as a university. In a focused and systematic way we have, together, made some fundamental difference for good in the lives of our neighbors on all sides. In schools and churches, clinics, neighborhood centers and renovated housing, Duke people are out there every day working with our neighbors as partners.

We are also involved with our city and county as partners in improving 'the quality of the society in which we live.' One of my colleagues is fond of reminding folks that Duke isn't going to be moving anywhere else. And I have no doubt that we will continue to be part of the solution to problems we face, and join in celebrating the many advantages of this vibrant region."

—NANNERL O. KEOHANE, *in her Founders' Day address in her last year as president*

*As of 2024, the **Duke-Durham Neighborhood Partnership** encompasses 14 neighborhoods and is administered by Duke's Office of Durham and Community Affairs. At right is the Durham childhood home of the feminist author and legal scholar, the Rev. Dr. Pauli Murray. The Duke Human Rights Center@Franklin Humanities Institute helped to nominate the house for its designation as a National Historic Landmark in 2016.*

CHAMPIONS

Vanessa Webb '99 is often described as the best women's tennis player ever to compete at Duke. Webb was the 1998 NCAA women's singles champion—the first Duke women's tennis player to win a national title. Named the ITA Player of the Year in 1998 and 1999, Webb was an All-America and an All-ACC selection all four years at Duke (1996–99) and was inducted into the Duke Athletics Hall of Fame in 2011.

In 1999, the **Duke women's golf** team broke through and claimed its first NCAA crown—and the first women's team national championship in school history. As of 2024, the team has seven national titles—more than any other team at Duke.

ADVANCING HEALTH

Duke physicians and medical researchers made profound contributions to health in the '90s. Also during this decade, infrastructure grew to enable Duke to serve more patients. **Ralph Snyderman**, M.D., served as chancellor for health affairs and dean of the School of Medicine from 1989 to 2004 and led Duke to become an internationally recognized leader in academic medicine.

93

Duke researchers identify apolipoprotein E (apoE) as the major susceptibility gene for Alzheimer's disease—and as one of many genetic risk factors for disease identified at Duke

◄

Duke pediatric immunologist **Louise Markert**, M.D., Ph.D., develops the first successful **thymus transplant**—the first treatment of its kind for babies suffering from thymus abnormalities

▼

Duke enrolls the final patient in GUSTO-I, at the time the largest clinical trial conducted in the United States

94

The Medical Center embarks on the busiest period of new construction in decades, including the Levine Science Research Center, Medical Sciences Research Building, a complete renovation of Duke Clinic, additions to the Morris Building for cancer care and research, a new Children's Health Center (above), a new ambulatory care building, and new parking garages

92

Duke Comprehensive Cancer Center develops the nation's first outpatient bone marrow transplantation program

Duke performs its first lung transplant *and its* first heart/lung transplant

Blake S. Wilson B.S.E.'74, Ph.D.'15, director of the **Duke Hearing Center**, develops innovations in signal processing for cochlear implants

90

Duke geneticists *invent a three-minute test to screen newborns for over 30 metabolic diseases at once — now routinely used throughout the country*

The **GUSTO Steering Committee** gathers for the release of the results from GUSTO-III, 1993.

1990s

October 7 1994 cover of Science. Reprinted with permission from AAS.

96

The Duke Clinical Research Institute *is established to conduct large, multinational clinical trials and perform outcomes research*

95

Duke scientists help discover the BRCA1 and BRCA2 genes, *which are responsible for many inherited forms of breast and ovarian cancers. Their findings were published in* **Science** *in 1994.*

▲

Duke cardiologist **Robert Califf** *'73, M.D.'78 served as executive director of the Duke Clinical Research Institute (DCRI) for its first 10 years. Califf would go on to serve twice as commissioner of the U.S. Food and Drug Administration (FDA).*

98

Duke University Health System *is created as Duke established partnerships with Durham Regional Hospital (now Duke Regional Hospital), Raleigh Community Hospital (now Duke Raleigh Hospital), and other regional healthcare providers and practices*

2000s | A DECADE *in* RETROSPECT

00

Same-sex unions *are officially celebrated in Duke Chapel*

McGovern-Davison Children's Health Center *opens, bringing all of Duke's pediatric specialties under one roof*
▼

01

Six Duke alumni die in the terrorist attacks of **September 11** *—a year later, a memorial grove is planted outside Keohane Quad*

James Bonk, *Ph.D., steps down from teaching general chemistry, a course he had taught since 1959 to over 30,000 Duke students, who fondly called it "Bonkistry"*

02

Women's Initiative *launched*

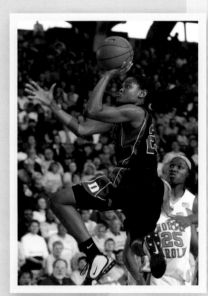

03

Duke-NUS Medical School *established*

04

▲

Richard H. Brodhead, *Ph.D., becomes Duke's ninth president*

Victor J. Dzau, *M.D., becomes chancellor for health affairs and president and CEO of the Duke University Health System (DUHS)*

Fitzpatrick Center for Interdisciplinary Engineering, Medicine and Applied Sciences *(CIEMAS) opens*

◄

Alana Beard *'04 becomes the first Duke women's basketball player to have her jersey retired*

Raleigh Community Hospital becomes **Duke Raleigh Hospital**

05

Bostock Library *and* **von der Heyden Pavilion** *open*

Duke selected to lead $300 million research consortium called the **Center for HIV/AIDS Vaccine Immunology** *(CHAVI)*

Nasher Museum of Art *opens*
▼

06

Duke Islamic Studies Center *(DISC) created*

The **Duke University School of Nursing** *enrolls the first students into its new doctoral degree program*

Duke Global Health Institute *established*

*Former president **Bill Clinton** attends the memorial service for Duke historian John Hope Franklin.*

07   **08**   **09**

DukeEngage *launches*

Paula D. McClain *becomes the first Black person to serve as chair of the Academic Council*

Office of Durham and Regional Affairs *created*

Latino/a Studies in the Global South program *begins*

John Hope Franklin *dies*

Center for Muslim Life *opens*
▼

The Sanford School of Public Policy *becomes Duke's tenth school*
▼

"Education is about becoming, about guided transformation. It stands to reason, therefore, that we should give deliberate thought to how female students at Duke become women, and how we can help them become the strongest, most fulfilled women they can possibly be." —NAN KEOHANE

00s

Victor J. Dzau, *James B. Duke Distinguished Professor of Medicine.*

President Nan Keohane *(center, in blue) pictured in 2000 with (left to right)* **Jean O'Barr**, *Ph.D., professor and founding director of Women's Studies at Duke;* **Lisa Lee** *Ph.D.'99; trustee emerita* **Judy Woodruff** *'68, Hon.'98, host of the* PBS NewsHour; **Eleanor Smeal** *'61, former president of the National Organization for Women; and philanthropist and Duke trustee emerita* **Melinda French Gates** *'86, M.B.A.'87, Hon.'13.*

In 2002, President Nan Keohane launched the Women's Initiative. Students, faculty, employees, alumnae, and trustees were interviewed about their experiences at Duke and the challenges they faced. The comprehensive report, which drew interest on campus and nationally, shared data, offered analyses, and made thoughtful policy recommendations. The Women's Initiative resulted in a number of tangible benefits to the university community. Duke created a leadership development program for undergraduate women, named the Baldwin Scholars for Alice Mary Baldwin, first dean of the Woman's College. Duke also implemented a $2-million expansion of Duke's on-site childcare center, plus additional childcare subsidies; a three-week paid parental leave for staff, which was increased to six weeks in 2020; guidelines for flexible work arrangements; and a new commitment to pay equity.

Richard H. Brodhead became Duke's ninth president in 2004. Brodhead came to Duke from Yale, where he had earned his undergraduate degree and Ph.D. and had had a 32-year career, including 11 years as dean of Yale College. A scholar of American literature and culture, Brodhead championed the idea of knowledge in service to society and expanded students' opportunities to engage with the world as part of their education.

Brodhead found an able lieutenant in **Peter Lange**, Ph.D., a political scientist who had been Duke's provost since 1999. Lange led the development and implementation of two strategic plans that identified interdisciplinary research and teaching as a key focus that could leverage many of Duke's strengths. Civic engagement, too, received new attention, and Duke began to interact with policymakers through such new centers as the Social Science Research Institute, the Nicholas Institute for Environmental Policy Solutions, and the Duke Institute for Brain Sciences.

Also arriving at Duke in 2004 was **Victor J. Dzau**, a distinguished cardiologist who became chancellor for health affairs and president and CEO of the Duke University Health System (DUHS). Dzau similarly looked toward the horizons, and bold international initiatives took shape in this decade.

The Duke University School of Medicine had been invited by the Government of Singapore to form a partnership. Grounded in Duke's research-intensive medical curriculum and fueled by Singapore's ambitions in the biomedical sciences, Duke and the National University of Singapore formed the Duke-NUS Medical School, which enrolled its first students in 2005. The next year, Duke launched the Global Health Institute to promote education, research, and service in health care to underserved populations globally.

Back on campus, two facilities opened in 2005 that exemplified Duke's new vision for its libraries, emphasizing its role in providing world-class resources and collaborative learning spaces. The five-story

2000s

Bostock Library offered a new technology hub and flexible study spaces, and the von der Heyden Pavilion created such an inviting café that student use of the library increased by 40 percent.

In 2006, the Duke and Durham communities experienced a painful chapter when three members of the men's lacrosse team were falsely accused of rape by a Durham woman. The accusations drew a storm of national media attention as the tinderbox of race, sex, and privilege became a flashpoint for Duke, Durham, and the nation. The charges against the men were eventually dismissed, the players exonerated, and the prosecuting attorney charged with withholding exculpatory evidence and jailed. He eventually surrendered his law license in the face of disbarment.

Following that episode Duke launched two new initiatives focused on local community relations that aimed to heal and enhance understanding between Duke and the larger Durham community. First, with support from The Duke Endowment and Duke alumna **Melinda French Gates**, Duke launched what would quickly become a signature community service program—DukeEngage.

Duke also established the Office of Durham and Regional Affairs to expand and deepen the university's engagement with the City of Durham, Durham Public Schools, local neighborhoods, and nonprofits. **Phail Wynn Jr.**, Ph.D., who had just retired as president of Durham Technical Community College, was named the office's first leader and brought his political savvy, strong networks, and personal warmth to his new role.

After a long economic downturn caused by the departure of tobacco manufacturing, the City of Durham was beginning to reinvent itself as a site of innovation and entrepreneurship. Duke began to partner with the city and developers on projects and to invest in key attractions such as the Durham Performing Arts Center, or DPAC. With these highly successful initiatives, the city and the university began to find a new way forward together. ■

*The Duke community paused to commemorate the **9/11 attacks** one year later, and a memorial grove was planted behind Keohane Quad.*

These trees were planted on
September 11, 2002 in memory of
the Duke graduates killed in the
terrorist attacks one year earlier.

A. Todd Rancke '81
Michael Morgan Taylor '81
John Robinson "Rob" Lenoir '84
Peter Keith Ortale '87
Christopher Todd Pitman '93
Frederick Charles Richnele III M.D. '94

A memorial plaque *by a grove of six trees planted behind Keohane Quad honors the six Duke alumni who were killed in the attacks on September 11, 2001.*

Students in a residency of the Weekend Executive MBA program in the **Fuqua School of Business** participate in an Integrative Leadership Experience (ILE).

Researchers with Duke's **Organization for Tropical Studies** conduct comparative ecosystem studies at Palo Verde, one of three biological field stations in Costa Rica.

LEGEND

JOHN HOPE FRANKLIN

John Hope Franklin, Ph.D., was James B. Duke Professor of History and Professor of Legal History in the Law School. In the 1940s, he conducted research at Duke for his book From Slavery to Freedom, the seminal work on African American history, which was first published in 1947. Franklin taught at St. Augustine College, North Carolina College (now N.C. Central University), Howard University, Brooklyn College, and the University of Chicago before being hired at Duke in 1984. President Bill Clinton awarded him the Presidential Medal of Freedom in 1995 and spoke at his memorial service in Duke Chapel in 2009. At Duke, there are several entities named for Franklin: the **John Hope Franklin Center for Interdisciplinary and International Studies**; the **Franklin Humanities Institute**; and the **John Hope Franklin Research Center for African American History and Culture.**

"*This is the work of a great university: the struggle to expand the domain of knowledge, the struggle to share that knowledge through education, and the struggle to put that knowledge to profound human use.*"

—Richard H. Brodhead, from his inaugural address, September 18, 2004

WELCOME ADDRESS

"*Duke has succeeded* in drawing top talent in a hundred forms from across every known social boundary—regional, national, racial, cultural, religious, political, socioeconomic, and more. As sociologists of knowledge have long recognized, from Renaissance Florence to the startup hotspots of today, the places where smart, energetic people from different starting points have been drawn together and allowed freely to collide have been the places where world-changing ideas are hatched and new human energies released. Today you become a citizen of just such a place. From today, every one of you will contribute to the dynamism of a massively diverse community, and everyone will get a growth boost from the others here with you.

You could not insulate yourself from this energy if you tried. But if you want to build to your full potential, you're going to have to use this resource in an intentional fashion, seek out and open yourself to this human richness, even if that means venturing outside what's comfortable. After the first diversity buzz wears off, you'll face inevitable temptations to fall back on communities that you subliminally perceive as "like you." And in even the healthiest communities, things can happen that pull people back from the things they share.

Duke is committed to being a community where everyone is respected and has an equal right to thrive. Therefore, Duke requires that each of you take responsibility to build such a community, treating every other with the respect that you wish for yourself. But since no human world could guarantee you a life free from all social ills, if frictions do arise, I hope you will find a more constructive way to engage with differences than recoiling in resentment or withdrawing in defensiveness, human as both impulses powerfully are. In this country and around the world, we see the price millions pay when differences harden into conflict and estrangement. Let's do better than that at Duke. Let's make it be part of your education to learn how to enter into points of view fundamentally different from your own and open your own point of view to those not already equipped to grasp it, and to practice this hard human skill not just on good days but even in times of challenge. This will make Duke a better place and will equip you to be a constructive social contributor long after you leave this place behind." ∎

—**President Richard H. Brodhead**, from "Constructing Duke," welcome address at Opening Convocation, August 19, 2015

GLOBAL EDUCATION

"Few experiences in my recent life have been as powerful as visiting Duke students in DukeEngage—young Duke engineers figuring out how to fix broken medical equipment in health clinics in rural Tanzania, or a young woman who, having studied Chinese at Duke, served as a teacher in a school for migrant children in Beijing. This is no extracurricular activity or summer pastime. This is education: a chance to learn the conditions of human life as they are lived outside the bubble of an elite American college campus, and a chance to discover how skills learned abstractly in academic settings can be applied and augmented in the world of human need."

—**RICHARD H. BRODHEAD,** president of Duke University and William Preston Few Professor of English, 2004–17

One long-standing DukeEngage program works with the **WISER school,** *which empowers underprivileged girls and their community in rural Kenya. Dancing is a key part of the school, and these Duke student participants came together on a bluff overlooking Lake Victoria to "leap for joy" together.*

DUKEENGAGE

Launched in 2007, DukeEngage gives undergraduates the opportunity to put their classroom learning in service to society through eight-week, faculty-led immersive programs focused on critical needs in the U.S. and around the world.

In the summer of 2023, nearly 400 Duke students had transformative experiences through 20 different DukeEngage programs—including working on sustainable development in Brazil, building a bridge in Eswatini, and empowering girls through STEM education in Orange County, California. ∎

The Duke-NUS Medical School *opened in 2005 as a partnership with the National University of Singapore. The first 26 students enrolled in the Doctor of Medicine (M.D.) degree.*

Will Mitchell, Ph.D. (center, in blue), professor of international management and strategy and **Duke Global Health Institute** *affiliate, led a program to help Nigerian partners build a sustainable model for health management training.*

2000s

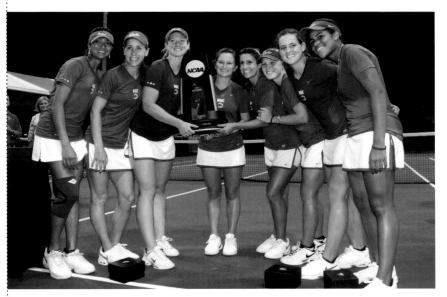

Women's tennis *won the national championship in 2009.*

The **Duke Pep Band** *began to play Cascada's "Everytime We Touch" in the 2006–07 season. The song quickly became a beloved anthem in Cameron Indoor Stadium.*

Students in Spanish language courses visited the Miró exhibition at the **Nasher Museum of Art** *(above).*

The NASHER MUSEUM of ART

Raymond D. Nasher *graduated from Duke in 1943 believing that art should be part of undergraduate education. He became one of the country's leading collectors of modern and contemporary sculpture and served on the university's Board of Trustees from 1968 through 1974. While Duke had had a small museum of art on campus since 1969, Nasher's generous gift in 1998 allowed Duke to contemplate building a new art museum and commission world-renowned architect Rafael Viñoly to design it. The resulting* **Nasher Museum of Art,** *which opened in 2005, changed the cultural landscape of the university and the region. With its 13,000-square-foot glass and steel canopy over the central gallery space, the Nasher offers an inviting space for students, faculty, staff, and the community, with three large galleries, an auditorium, classrooms, a museum shop, and a café with outdoor seating overlooking a sculpture garden.*

Interior of the **Nasher Museum of Art**

Construction projects *in the 2000s included (clockwise from top left): The Fitzpatrick Center for Interdisciplinary Engineering, Medicine and Applied Sciences (CIEMAS); the French Family Science Center; the von der Heyden Pavilion in Perkins Library, home to a café called The Perk; and the Duke Children's Hospital and Health Center.*

The von der Heyden Pavilion is named for trustee emeritus **Karl von der Heyden '62** *and his wife,* **Mary Ellen**, *who have provided generous support across the university, including for the arts, libraries, and the Duke Global Health Institute.*

2010s | A DECADE *in* RETROSPECT

Duke Kunshan University *opened its doors to students in 2014.*

10

Duke Campus Farm *established*

Duke men's lacrosse *team wins the first of three national championships*

11

Reynolds Price, *James B. Duke Professor of English, dies*

The Duke Endowment *gives Duke $80 million to fund renovations of the West Union building and Page and Baldwin auditoriums*

12

Mary Duke Biddle Trent Semans *dies*

The Duke Forward *campaign launches publicly—it is the largest capital campaign in the university's history*

13

Duke commemorates the fiftieth anniversary of the enrollment of the first five Black undergraduates

Bass Connections *launches with a gift from trustee Anne Bass and her husband, Bob Bass*

The Mary Duke Biddle Trent Semans Center for Health Education *opens*

Durham Regional Hospital becomes Duke Regional Hospital

Baldwin Auditorium *reopens after renovations*

14

Duke Kunshan University *(DKU) enrolls its first graduate students*

Sally Kornbluth, *Ph.D., becomes provost*

Blue Devils United *is created, representing Duke's LQBTQIA+ community*

15

Men's basketball wins its fifth national championship and adds a fifth banner to Cameron Indoor Stadium

Duke-Margolis Center for Health Policy *launches with a gift from Duke alumnus Robert J. Margolis M.D.'71*

A. Eugene Washington, *M.D., becomes chancellor for health affairs and president and CEO of Duke University Health System*

*Trustee emeritus **Bruce Karsh '77** also served as chair of the Board of DUMAC, LLC, the entity that manages the Duke University endowment, from 2005 to 2014. Bruce and Martha Karsh have provided major support for financial aid and access at Duke. The Karsh International Scholars Program and the Karsh Office of Undergraduate Financial Support were named in recognition of their gifts to Duke.*

16

17

18

19

West Union reopens after extensive renovations, later renamed the Richard H. Brodhead Center for Campus Life

*West Campus Quad is renamed **Abele Quad** in honor of architect Julian Abele*

Vincent E. Price, Ph.D., becomes the tenth president of Duke University

DKU enrolls its first undergraduate students

Rubenstein Arts Center ("the Ruby") opens

Karsh Alumni and Visitors Center opens

Duke Science and Technology initiative launches to elevate and sustain excellence in the sciences

*2012: Duke professor **Robert Lefkowitz**, M.D., wins the **Nobel Prize in Chemistry** along with his former postdoctoral fellow **Brian Kobilka**, M.D., for their work with G protein-coupled receptors*

*2015: Duke professor **Paul Modrich**, Ph.D., wins the **Nobel Prize in Chemistry** for his discoveries on DNA repair*

*Financier and philanthropist **David Rubenstein '70** served as chair of the Duke University Board of Trustees from 2013 to 2017. His generous support has enriched many areas at Duke, including the arts, libraries, athletics, financial aid, and Jewish Life at Duke. In addition to "the Ruby," Rubenstein Hall, the Rubenstein Scholars program, and the David M. Rubenstein Rare Book & Manuscript Library are named in his honor.*

Paul Modrich *(right), professor of biochemistry and Howard Hughes Medical Investigator, won the Nobel Prize in Chemistry in 2015 for his work on DNA repair. He was honored in Cameron Indoor Stadium along with* Robert J. Lefkowitz *(left), who won the 2012 Nobel Prize in Chemistry with his former postdoctoral fellow* Brian Kobilka, *M.D., for their work with G protein-coupled receptors. Lefkowitz currently serves as the Chancellor's Distinguished Professor of Medicine and Professor of Biochemistry and Chemistry at Duke and has been an Investigator of the Howard Hughes Medical Institute since 1976.*

10s

Duke seniors Jay Ruckelshaus and Laura Roberts were named **Rhodes Scholars** *in 2015—two of the seven Duke students who received the award in the 2010s.*

The 2010s at Duke were a decade of growth and expansion. The Duke Forward campaign held its public launch in 2012, announcing a campaign that aimed to raise $3.25 billion and would eventually bring in $3.85 billion.

With a gift of $80 million in 2011, The Duke Endowment put Duke's plans to revitalize the campus in motion—transforming West Union and renovating Page Auditorium on West Campus and Baldwin Auditorium on East Campus. At the time, the grant was the largest single philanthropic gift in the history of the university and the Endowment.

Baldwin Auditorium re-opened in 2013 to rave reviews from musicians and audiences alike as its superb acoustics made it one of the premier small venues for classical music in the Southeast. Even more dramatic was the transformation of the West Union building. With careful attention paid to preserving the historic exterior while modernizing the interior, the newly brightened and dynamic space re-opened in 2016 and was renamed the Richard H. Brodhead Center for Campus Life in 2017.

Together with renovations to Duke Chapel and the Libraries, the transformation of Duke's central common spaces offered rich new opportunities for both the Duke and Durham communities. The cumulative effect was to render the campus more inviting and welcoming and facilitate both intentional and fortuitous interactions among faculty, staff, and students as well as members of the community.

In the 2010s, Duke faculty and students garnered extraordinary recognition for their work. Two members of the School of Medicine faculty—**Robert Lefkowitz** in 2012 and **Paul Modrich** in 2015—won the Nobel Prize in Chemistry. They were the first Nobel Prizes awarded for research done by Duke faculty on the Duke campus.

During Brodhead's tenure as president, nine undergraduates were named Rhodes Scholars; applications for undergraduate admission nearly doubled, from 16,702 in 2004 to more than 32,000 in 2016; and Duke's athletic teams won 10 national championships as student-athletes achieved a 98 percent graduation rate.

The ranks of senior leadership at Duke also became more diverse in important ways. Brodhead oversaw the appointments of **Paula D. McClain** as dean of The Graduate School in 2012; the **Rev. Dr. Luke A. Powery** as dean of Duke Chapel in 2012; and **A. Eugene Washington** as chancellor for health affairs in 2015. They were the first Black individuals to hold their respective positions. And in 2018, the provost and eight of the 10 deans of the schools at Duke were women.

The Duke Forward campaign strengthened Duke's commitment to access and opportunity, raising nearly $1 billion for financial aid endowment. It also fueled new curricular innovations. Launched in 2013, **Bass Connections**, named in honor of founding donors **Anne T. and Robert M. Bass** P'97, imagined a new model of experiential learning that brought together faculty and students to explore pressing

Sally Kornbluth, *James B. Duke Professor of Pharmacology and Cancer Biology and vice dean for the School of Medicine, was named provost in 2014. Kornbluth was the first woman to serve as Duke's chief academic officer. She succeeded **Peter Lange**, whose 15-year tenure made him the longest serving provost in Duke history. In 2022, Kornbluth was named president of the Massachusetts Institute of Technology (MIT).*

Phail Wynn, Jr., *vice president for Durham and Regional Affairs, and* **Tallman Trask III**, *executive vice president.*

*Launched in 2012, the **Duke Forward campaign** raised $3.85 billion over seven years to benefit Duke's graduate and undergraduate schools, athletics, libraries, Duke Health, and a range of university-wide initiatives and programs. Funds have been used to transform the campus and advance priorities, including financial aid, faculty development, research and patient care, and hands-on learning opportunities for students.*

societal challenges through interdisciplinary research and education.

Also in the 2010s, downtown Durham was experiencing a renaissance, and Duke played a key role. Vice President of Durham and Regional Affairs **Phail Wynn Jr.** said that Duke went from being an "invisible hand" in Durham to a more active, visible community partner. Executive Vice President **Tallman Trask III**, Ph.D., led both the building boom on campus and Duke's investments in downtown Durham. At one point 3,500 Duke employees worked in downtown Durham in offices and laboratory spaces, amounting to more than one million square feet of leased space. This influx of working professionals helped to attract restaurants, shops, and other businesses that revitalized downtown Durham.

By 2017, construction projects were nearing completion, the Duke Forward campaign had smashed through its goal, and Brodhead stepped down after 13 years as president.

That year, **Vincent E. Price** became Duke's tenth president. A leading global expert on public opinion and political communication, he was appointed the Walter Hines Page Professor of Public Policy and Political Science in the Sanford School of Public Policy and Trinity College of Arts and Sciences. Price came to Duke from the University of Pennsylvania, where he had been provost for eight years.

In his first address to the faculty, Price posed two questions: "First:

what do we wish the Duke of tomorrow will be? And secondly, what steps will need to be taken to get there?" To answer those questions, he set forth the five core principles of his strategic vision: Duke must empower the boldest thinkers; transform teaching and learning; strengthen the campus community; partner with purpose in the region; and engage a global network of alumni.

Price's strategic vision began to find expression across the university. Price charged an Arts Planning Group to chart the future strategic direction for the arts at Duke, aiming to make the arts "both a vital point of connection amidst the rich diversity of our university community and a creative engine for discovery." Strategic task forces led by the Board of Trustees made key recommendations on residential life and the student experience as well as the alumni network, among other topics. Trustees were also engaged in making recommendations to strengthen research translation and commercialization and regional partnerships. With major support from The Duke Endowment, Price launched the Duke Science and Technology initiative, a university-wide effort to attract and retain top faculty in the sciences. In these ways and many others, Duke continued to lead, innovate, and connect with the surrounding community—and set the stage for important initiatives and decisions to come. ∎

*Civil and environmental engineering student Mona Dai did **DukeEngage** in Uganda in 2012, then went to Togo for a follow-up project in 2013— building a sanitation system that would also generate electricity and fertilizer.*

*Duke Environment Hall, now called **Grainger Hall**, opened in 2014 as the new home for the Nicholas School of the Environment and the hub of environmental activity on campus. The building earned LEED Platinum certification with its rooftop solar panels, innovative climate control and water systems, and sustainably designed landscaping.*

BASS CONNECTIONS

In the program's first decade, 5,500 members of the Duke community, including 3,440 undergraduates, took part in 830 Bass Connections yearlong project teams and summer research projects. Teams have worked in 46 countries on six continents and in more than 20 states.

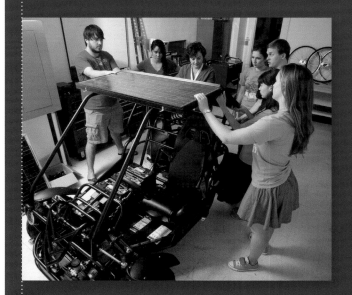

*Known for his eloquence and wit, Brodhead co-chaired a national Commission on the Humanities and Social Sciences and became a compelling spokesperson for the **value of a liberal arts education**. He appeared on* The Colbert Report *in 2013 to discuss the Commission's report and sparred playfully with comedian Stephen Colbert.*

***Emily Klein**, Ph.D., professor of Earth and Ocean Sciences in the Nicholas School, leads a Bass Connections project team called "Energy and the Environment: Design and Innovation" that built a solar-powered vehicle.*

A crane loomed over the campus as the West Union building was being transformed. The space was later named the **Richard H. Brodhead Center for Campus Life**.

BUILDINGS *of* SIGNIFICANCE

An enormous crane became a familiar sight while West Campus was under construction.

The **West Union building** *(now the Brodhead Center), formerly the home of the Cambridge Inn ("the C.I."), the University Room ("the U-Room"), and the Great Hall ("the Pits"), underwent a dramatic transformation and once again became the hub of Duke student life. The renovation preserved the historic exterior that faces Abele Quad and the signature dining hall spaces while re-envisioning the interior with modern glass and steel, catwalks, and skylights.*

Rubenstein Library made major upgrades for the preservation of and access to Duke's special collections and revitalized the iconic **Gothic Reading Room***.*

The restoration of **Baldwin Auditorium** *won awards for historic preservation.*

The **Rubenstein Arts Center***, nicknamed "the Ruby," opened its doors in January 2018. Named in recognition of a gift from trustee emeritus and former board chair David M. Rubenstein '70, the Ruby hosts courses, rehearsals, performances, and public arts programs. The Ruby also regularly hosts visiting artists such as the American Ballet Theatre Studio Company and has become a popular home for American Dance Festival classes and performances.*

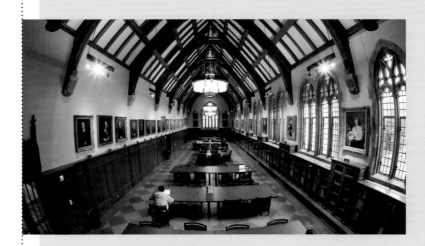

New buildings and renovations breathed new life into the campus, including **Baldwin Auditorium** *(top), the* **Rubenstein Arts Center** *(bottom), and the* **Gothic Reading Room** *(right).*

TRIUMPH

*Under head coach **John Danowski, Duke men's lacrosse** has won three national championships (2010, 2013, and 2014). Danowski arrived at Duke in 2006 and is the winningest coach in Division I men's lacrosse history. He was inducted into the National Lacrosse Hall of Fame in 2023.*

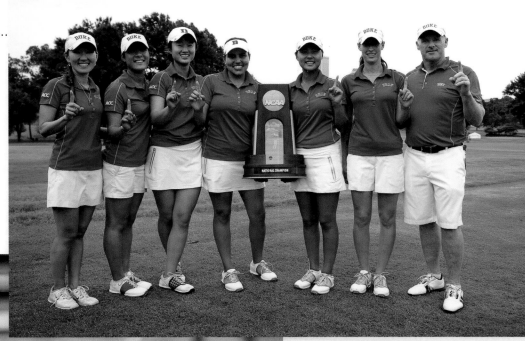

The women's golf team *won the national championship in 2014. As of 2024, the team has won **seven national titles**—the most of any team at Duke.*

2010s

Coach **David Cutcliffe** and the football team celebrate after beating Indiana 44–41 in overtime in the **Pinstripe Bowl** in Yankee Stadium on December 27, 2015. It was Duke's first bowl win since 1961.

The **men's basketball** team celebrates after winning the 2015 national championship.

2010s

Mary Duke Biddle Trent Semans '39 served on the Duke University Board of Trustees from 1961 to 1981. She also spent decades as a trustee, vice chair, and chair of The Duke Endowment, the private foundation founded by her great-uncle James B. Duke. Semans was also devoted to her adopted hometown of Durham. She served as mayor pro tem of Durham and from 1948 to 1976 was a trustee of Lincoln Community Hospital, a facility the Duke family started in 1901 to serve the needs of Black patients in Durham.

"The granddaughter of Benjamin N. Duke and the great-granddaughter of Washington Duke, she was an irrepressible force for good in Duke, Durham, and the region, and when she died at age 92, the outpouring for her was unforgettable."
—Richard H. Brodhead, from *Speaking of Duke*

The **Trent Semans Center for Health Education** *was the first new home for medical education at Duke since 1930.*

*The **Duke Cancer Center** building opened in 2012. Staff and patients provided input to create "a physical embodiment of Duke Cancer's philosophy of patient-centered care." Pictured is the Duke Cancer Center interior and atrium.*

*Closed for a year for renovations, **Duke Chapel** reopened in May 2016.*

In August 2017, the statue of Robert E. Lee in the portal of Duke Chapel was removed at the direction of President Price following its defacement a few days earlier. After a year of deliberation, it was decided that the niche that once held the statue would remain empty. A plaque inside the Chapel explains the reasoning, quoting the **Rev. Dr. Luke A. Powery** *(above)*, dean of Duke Chapel, who said that the empty space might represent "a hole that is in the heart of the United States of America, and perhaps in our own human hearts—that hole that is from the sin of racism and hatred of any kind."

2010s

In October 2016, the **Board of Trustees named the entire West Campus quad for Julian Abele,** *the Black architect who designed the campus in the 1920s. Four generations of the Abele family attended the dedication ceremony for Abele Quad.*

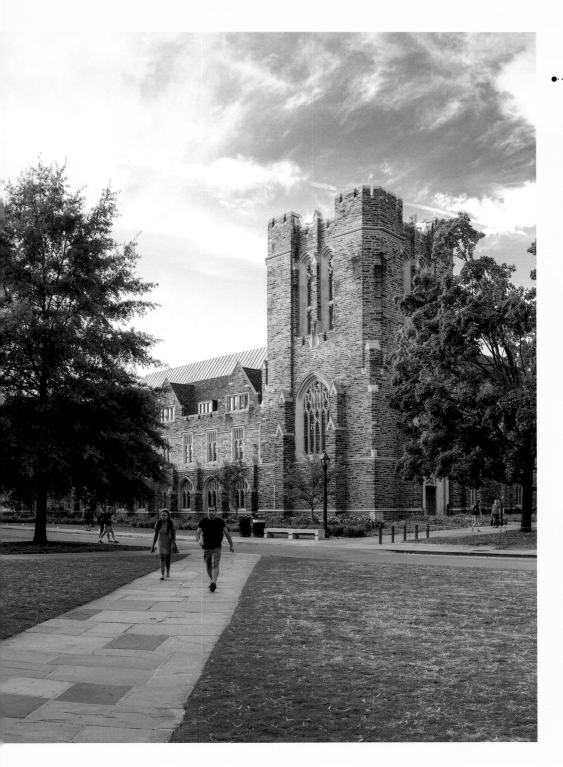

Gene Kendall, Wilhelmina Reuben-Cooke, *and* **Nathaniel "Nat" White Jr.** *attended commemoration events in 2013 to mark the fiftieth anniversary of their enrollment. At the time, they were the three surviving members of the* **first five Black undergraduate students to integrate the university.**

In 2018, the Board of Trustees voted to remove the name of Julian S. Carr from a classroom building on East Campus. Carr, a Durham businessman and a trustee of Trinity College, had donated the land upon which **East Campus** *was built as part of the effort to move Trinity to Durham in the early 1890s. The history department, which is housed in the building, had proposed to remove the name because of Carr's documented promotion of white supremacy.*

VOICES

PRESIDENT VINCENT E. PRICE,
Inaugural Address, **October 5, 2017**

"*We are, finally, called upon today* to renew our commitment to healing and to serving our surrounding communities. At each key moment of institutional regeneration, our predecessors understood and reconfirmed their obligation to marshal Duke's teaching, learning, and discovery to positive social ends, and so we do today. We heal human injuries and illnesses; we work to heal division within our own community; and we use our skills and knowledge to aid healing and reconciliation elsewhere. We serve our fellow students and colleagues, our local community, and the world beyond to improve life and well-being for others.

This work begins here on campus. Our new century demands that we prepare ourselves for a diverse and often chaotic world, whose challenges, controversies, and crises do not stop at Duke's gates. We need to work together to defend—even seek out—voices that are different from our own. This is hard work, but if we are to heal the divisions in the world we have to open ourselves, honestly and deeply, to a diversity of perspectives.

One great advantage Duke has in this work is that we are part of a vibrantly global community. But we must be careful not to overlook the challenges and opportunities in our own backyard. James B. Duke called on us, in his words, to "develop our resources, increase our wisdom, and promote human happiness." The truest tests of our commitment to healing and serving, the most accurate gauges of our resolve, are right here in North Carolina.

We have done much over the past decade to strengthen our service to this city and region. And yet, much good work remains.

Are we bold enough to consciously work to break down the division between what we do regionally and what we do globally? Are we humble enough to understand that we need not travel to the other side of the world to find communities in need, both rural and urban, or willing partners with whom we can work to propel human welfare, creativity, and fulfillment?

Our new century calls for a university that grounds its ambition to heal and serve the world in humility; that confronts its own problems as readily as it does others'; and that shows its most generous and supportive self to its own neighborhood.

I believe Duke can and will be that university." ∎

At the **Duke University Marine Lab** in Beaufort, N.C., Daniel Rittschof, Ph.D., gives President Price a quick lesson in crab behavioral biology.

Dr. DAN

2020s

A DECADE *in* RETROSPECT

20

In response to the COVID-19 pandemic, classes transition to remote instruction, labs are shuttered, many faculty and staff begin working remotely, and Duke Health providers focus on caring for patients with COVID-19

▸ Kara Lawson *hired as head coach of women's basketball*

Jarvis Hall, named for Thomas Jarvis, a Trinity alumnus with ties to the 1898 Wilmington Massacre, renamed West Residence Hall

▸

Racial Equity Advisory Council *formed*

21

University Carillonneur **J. Samuel Hammond '68,** *M.T.S. '96, who played the bells in Duke Chapel for more than 50 years, dies; the carillon is later named for him*

Sociology-Psychology Building on West Campus renamed for the late trustee emerita **Wilhelmina Reuben-Cooke '67**

World's first *combination heart transplant–thymus procedure performed at Duke*

Nina King *named vice president and director of athletics, the first woman and person of color to hold the position*

▸

22   **23**   **24**

Coach Mike Krzyzewski
retires *after 42 years; Jon
Scheyer becomes head
coach of men's basketball*

*A new minor is established
in the* **Asian American
and Diaspora Studies**
program

QuadEx *begins as the
new residential model*

World's first *partial heart
transplant performed at
Duke*
◀

Duke launches its
Climate Commitment
▶

*The Duke Endowment
awards Duke University*
$100 million *in
recognition of the shared
centennial of the two
institutions; the gift
includes support for
financial aid for students
from the Carolinas*

Duke celebrates its Centennial

100

Ben Cooke, *Ph.D., teaches students in
Engineering 101 in a classroom set up outside.*

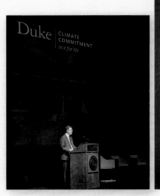

*Kevin Bierlich Ph.D.'21 and Walter Torres Ph.D.'21 measured whales near
Antarctica as part of the* **Duke Marine Robotics and Remote Sensing Lab**.

20s

Because of the COVID-19 pandemic, no fans were allowed in Cameron Indoor Stadium for men's or women's basketball games during the 2020–21 season. Printed graphics in the bleachers depicted the **Cameron Crazies** instead.

◄ Anusha Vojjola M.Eng.M.'22 asks a question on the first day of class in Spring 2021. In the class, which is taught by Professor Steven DelGrosso in the new **Wilkinson Building**, half of the students attend in person and half are remote.

Everyone who was at Duke in early 2020 remembers the email dated March 10, 2020, sent by President Vincent Price. The COVID-19 pandemic had emerged as a global threat. Students were instructed not to return to campus following spring break; all classes would transition to online and virtual formats. Over the next few weeks, labs were shuttered, many faculty and staff began remote work, and all travel and events were canceled. Duke University Health System remained open and continued caring for all patients, including those infected with COVID.

In this new and unprecedented world, Duke rapidly began to develop and implement a comprehensive strategy that prioritized continuation of the core missions of the university—teaching, research, service, and clinical care—while protecting the health and safety of Duke students, faculty, and staff as well as the Durham community. Over the next three years, Duke would draw on the expertise of dedicated faculty and staff across the university and health system who pooled their knowledge in virology, immunology, epidemiology, public health, psychology, sociology, and many other fields. Through the anxiety of the pandemic, Duke faculty and staff rose to the challenge to enable the university to remain open, serve the community, and contribute to the understanding of the new coronavirus and its global impact.

In the summer of 2020, a new crisis gripped the nation. The murder of George Floyd by a white police officer in Minneapolis put a new spotlight on systemic racism and injustice and resulted in widespread pain and trauma for many Americans. Black Lives Matter protests erupted across the country.

Duke also responded in powerful ways. In a message for Juneteenth of 2020, President Price committed the university at "every level of institutional activity" to "take transformative action now toward eliminating the systems of racism and inequality that have shaped the lived experiences of too many members of the Duke community." Duke Health launched "Moments to Movement," signifying its commitment to diversity, inclusion, and equity and its determination to enact lasting change.

In August 2020, hundreds of Duke student-athletes, coaches, and staff came together for a peaceful protest, led by men's basketball director of operations and player development **Nolan Smith** '11. "We're here today to talk about feelings," said Smith at the event. "There are Black student-athletes out here, there are white student-athletes out here, and we all have feelings right now. Unless it's addressed, you keep it bottled up, and you can't keep it bottled up because all that does is create anger, and we're all angry, sad, frustrated, and confused. We're here to talk about all that today."

Laurene Sperling '78 *was elected chair of the Duke University Board of Trustees in 2021. She is the first woman to serve as chair.*

EXECUTIVE LEADERSHIP TRANSITIONS *(left to right)*

Daniel Ennis *came from The Johns Hopkins University in 2020 to become Duke's executive vice president.*

Craig T. Albanese, *M.D., who joined the Duke University Health System as executive vice president and chief operating officer in 2022, was named chief executive officer in 2023.*

Alec D. Gallimore, *Ph.D., was announced in 2023 as Duke's provost and chief academic officer; he came from the University of Michigan, where he was the Robert J. Vlasic Dean of Engineering.*

Mary E. Klotman *'76, M.D.'80, H.S.'80–'85, was named Duke's first executive vice president for health affairs in 2023 while continuing to serve as dean of the School of Medicine.*

The Board of Trustees *is the governing body of Duke University, with a fiduciary responsibility to safeguard the long-term health of the university. The board works with Duke leaders to oversee the strategic direction of the university and works to ensure that educational policy, finances, and operations are aligned with its mission. The 37 members of the Board of Trustees include accomplished leaders from many different fields as well as three Young Trustees. The Young Trustee position was created by President Terry Sanford in 1972 to include voices who are closer to the student experience. Every year, one individual from the undergraduate student body and one individual from the graduate and professional student body are elected as Young Trustees.*

In the meantime, the COVID-19 pandemic was still raging. In the fall of 2020, as many American colleges and universities stayed closed, Duke became widely admired for its careful approach to allowing students back on campus. Duke developed an app to report symptoms, staffed a hotline for employees, implemented an approach to test all students on a regular basis, and devised a system of contact tracing. On-campus housing was limited to first-year and sophomore students only, and all rooms were single occupancy. The goal was to quickly identify any COVID-19 cases on campus and limit transmission. Over the next two years, more than 1.2 million COVID-19 tests of Duke students, faculty, and staff were processed by the Duke Human Vaccine Institute. A case study published by the Centers for Disease Control and Prevention (CDC) showed that the Duke approach was highly effective in preventing outbreaks and allowing the campus to remain open.

In December 2020, Duke University Hospital received its first shipment of the brand new COVID-19 vaccine, and onlookers cheered as **Faye Williams**, a retired nurse who had come back to work as a patient care coordinator during the pandemic, became the first person to receive the vaccine at Duke. Over the next two months, Duke Health would administer more than 100,000 doses to patients, staff, and members of the community.

For most of 2020 and into 2021, Duke University Medical Center physicians, nurses, providers, and staff continued to care for thousands of patients with many health issues, including COVID. The pandemic affected vulnerable populations disproportionately, and Duke partnered with community organizations to ensure information and access to care was available broadly. Duke researchers across campus pivoted their work to focus on the crisis at hand, and Duke was recognized for its innovation and as an international leader in COVID research to understand transmission, improve testing, develop new treatments, and inform health policy.

As vaccines became widely available, the Duke campus returned to full occupancy in the fall of 2021. Many faculty and staff returned to in-person work, while remote work continued as the norm for many. Students rejoiced to be back together on campus, and the lessening of restrictions meant that beloved traditions, such as gathering for the class photo and games in Cameron, could be revived. With life on campus returning to near-normalcy, the university began to advance the strategic vision that President Price had developed—to empower the boldest thinkers, transform teaching and

A Duke student-athlete takes part in the **Black Lives Matter** protest on campus on August 23, 2020.

learning, strengthen the campus community, partner with purpose in the community, and engage the global network of Duke alumni.

Here are just a few examples of how Duke is making progress toward these goals. The Duke Science and Technology initiative has recruited new faculty in science, medicine, technology, engineering, and mathematics. Innovative university courses enable undergraduates to make sense of complex societal issues from climate change to racial equity while learning from faculty from across the university. The Racial Equity Advisory Council, created in 2020, has worked to implement the goals of President Price's Juneteenth message. In 2022 Duke launched QuadEx, a new living and learning model, to foster a welcoming and inclusive community while supporting student well-being. And Duke is a thoughtful partner with the City of Durham and communities across North Carolina even as it connects with alumni around the world.

In 2024, as Duke celebrates its centennial, members of the Duke community are coming together to take pride in the achievements of the university's first 100 years, acknowledge the moments of challenge and growth, and look toward the promise of a new century. ■

"Life is precious. Most mornings, I awaken with a sense of gratitude and a renewed spirit, excited about the day ahead. The last few days, however, have been quite different. I have struggled to maintain my usual expectant energy and attitude. My heart has simply been heavy and overcome with sorrow, and like many of you, I have no words to ease this pain.

The unconscionable and senseless death of George Floyd in Minnesota, along with the appalling shootings of Ahmaud Arbery in Georgia and Breonna Taylor in Kentucky, leaves me overwhelmed and speechless. I am deeply troubled by the systemic racism and injustice that continue to plague our country and tear families apart. Like many of you, I am feeling vulnerable and afraid for my community, my colleagues, my friends, and my family. As a black man, these events hit particularly close to home."

—**Excerpt from a message to the Duke Health community, Monday, June 1, 2020 A. Eugene Washington, Chancellor for Health Affairs, Duke University President and CEO, Duke University Health System**

"Here at Duke, we aspire to be agents of progress in advancing racial equity and justice. . . . We have accomplished so much in which we take pride, and yet we have often been slow to do the right things, the hard things, the transformative things.

We must take transformative action now toward eliminating the systems of racism and inequality that have shaped the lived experiences of too many members of the Duke community.

We cannot, on this Juneteenth, bring news of true freedom—freedom from oppression, violence, and systemic racism. In many ways, even after a century and a half, that goal sadly remains elusive. But today, we can bring news of Duke's commitment to be partners on the path to achieving it."

—**Excerpt from President Vincent Price's Juneteenth message in 2020, announcing that Friday, June 19, 2020, would be a day of reflection for the entire Duke University community. The next year, Juneteenth became a national holiday.**

2020s

"This is an unprecedented challenge for our university community, but we are very well prepared to meet it. The same innovative spirit that has driven a century of Duke discoveries will allow our faculty, staff, and students to adapt to new teaching and learning experiences; the same commitment to service and courage demonstrated by Duke Health providers and staff every day will likewise carry us through these trying circumstances."

—**President Vincent E. Price, writing to the Duke community on March 10, 2020**

Creative learning spaces *during the pandemic.*

Duke physicians **Viviana Martinez-Bianchi,** *M.D., (left) and* **Gabriela Maradiaga Panayotti,** *M.D., helped to organize a team of doctors, nurses, and others to address local health disparities, particularly in the Latinx community. The group called itself the Latinx Advocacy Team & Interdisciplinary Network for COVID-19, or LATIN-19.*

Lana Wahid, *M.D., hugs Maury Turner as he heads home on August 14, 2020. Turner spent thirty-two days in a Duke Hospital ICU recovering from COVID-19. He was among a group of patients representing the combined total of* **1,000 discharged** *from* **Duke University Hospital, Duke Regional Hospital,** *and* **Duke Raleigh Hospital.**

"Looking back over the year, I am so grateful for our entire Duke community. You all have helped us to get our labs up and going again, to deliver patient care, and to continue our education. And everybody had to pull in the same direction to do that. . . ."

—**Mary E. Klotman, dean of the School of Medicine, in an April 2021 video illustrating the outstanding work by Duke faculty, staff, and students and offering thanks for their commitment and sacrifices in fulfilling the missions of excellence in patient care, research and discovery, education, and community service**

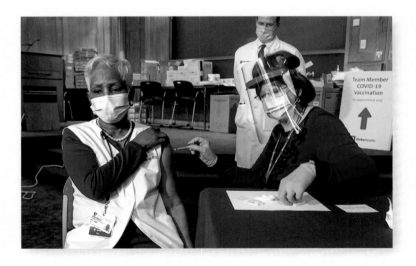

December 15, 2020, lifted spirits and offered hope as **Faye Williams** *was the first Duke employee to receive the COVID-19 vaccine at Duke Health. "I want to show that it is safe to take it," said Williams, who came out of retirement in 2020 to join Duke's efforts during the pandemic.*

COMMUNITY

In the spring, first-year students process to West Campus to be welcomed into the quads where they will live in their sophomore year. Under the **QuadEx** model, first-year residential communities are paired with a quad on West Campus to offer continuity across all four years at Duke.

When Duke Divinity School professor **Kate Bowler**, Ph.D., was diagnosed with stage IV cancer, her willingness to confront difficult truths about life resonated with many people going through challenges of their own. She shared her insights through a popular podcast and a series of best-selling books. A line from her book Everything Happens for a Reason: And Other Lies I've Loved became a mural in downtown Durham: "Life is so beautiful. Life is so hard."

2020s

CLIMATE

Launched in 2022, the **Duke Climate Commitment** *began a university-wide effort to marshal Duke's resources to address the climate crisis through education, research, external engagement, and campus operations.* **Toddi Steelman** *Ph.D.'96, formerly dean of the* **Nicholas School of the Environment***, was named vice president and vice provost, leading Duke's new Office of Climate and Sustainability. Moments before the Duke Climate Commitment announcement in Page Auditorium, President Vince Price fist bumps Steelman (below).*

LEGACY

At his press conference to announce that the **2021–22 season** *would be his final year of coaching,* **Mike Krzyzewski** *said, "My family and I view today as a celebration. Our time at both West Point and Duke has been beyond amazing, and we are thankful and honored to have led two college programs at world-class institutions for more than four decades."*

In **42** *seasons as head coach of Duke men's basketball, Krzyzewski created an indelible legacy:*

5 *national championships (1991, 1992, 2001, 2010, 2015)*

6 *gold medals as head coach of the U.S. Men's National Team*

12 *National Coach of the Year honors (eight seasons)*

13 *Final Four appearances (most in NCAA history)*

14 *ACC regular season championships*

15 *ACC Tournament championships (most in league history)*

101 *NCAA Tournament wins (most in NCAA history)*

1,129 *victories at Duke (most in NCAA history at one school)*

1,202 *career wins (most in the history of NCAA men's basketball)*

Former Duke All-American and two-time team captain **Jon Scheyer** *'10 became Duke's head coach beginning in the 2022–23 season. Scheyer graduated from Duke in 2010 and had served as associate head coach for three years. In Scheyer's first season as head coach, the Blue Devils notched a 27–9 record, went undefeated at home, and won the ACC Tournament.*

VOICES

VISION

"As we look ahead to our second century, our strategic vision is an invitation for all of us—faculty, students, staff, alumni, and friends of the university—to think together about our turn to the future, about how we can remain true to the Duke we have always been while charting our course toward the Duke we are destined to become.

Together, we will marshal our collective talents toward addressing the great challenges of our day, define a new twenty-first-century model of the research university, foster a more inclusive and equitable campus and world, partner with purpose in service to our community, and advance humankind. " **—President Vincent E. Price**

Chris Monroe, *Ph.D., Gilhuly Family Presidential Distinguished Professor, is an international leader in quantum computing with appointments in the Departments of Physics and Electrical and Computer Engineering.*

EMPOWERING *the* BOLDEST THINKERS

Launched with two **$50 million grants** *from The Duke Endowment, the Duke Science and Technology initiative is organized around themes that bridge the university and the health system: materials science, computing, and resilience of the body and brain.*

TRANSFORMING TEACHING *and* LEARNING

Beginning in the fall of 2022, Duke has offered **experiential orientation programs** *to all incoming first-year students.*

▼

2020s

STRENGTHENING *the* CAMPUS COMMUNITY

The Racial Equity Advisory Council, formed in 2020, works to promote **racial equity** at Duke through efforts to increase the diversity of the faculty, strengthen the campus community, and invest in staff development and training.

Under **QuadEx**, Duke's new inclusive living and learning model, first-year residence halls on East Campus have been linked with quads on West Campus to provide continuity of residential and social communities. Faculty-in-residence and faculty fellows are appointed to foster intellectual dimensions of residential life.

PARTNERING *with* PURPOSE

Duke's **Office of Durham and Community Affairs** coordinates community engagement efforts focused on college and career readiness, nonprofit capacity, housing affordability, early childhood education, and food security. **Beyond Durham**, Duke works to have a positive impact across North Carolina in education, collaborative research, service, and clinical care. Duke is also leading a new era of collaboration and innovation in the Research Triangle to grow a **supportive ecosystem for research translation and commercialization**.

ACTIVATING *the* GLOBAL NETWORK

Duke continues to offer **innovative lifelong learning opportunities** to alumni, working to strengthen its network of 180,000 Duke alumni around the world and changing what it means to be **"Forever Duke."**

Research associate **Graham H. Miller** (above) steps out of the mobile water reclaimer he and the **Duke Smart Toilet Lab** and **Center for WaSH-AID** teams fabricated for community outreach as part of Duke's effort to reinvent the standard toilet for safer water conservation in the United States and abroad.

ACKNOWLEDGMENTS

IT HAS BEEN A PRIVILEGE to be part of an amazing team that created this book, and I am indebted to the talent and dedication of many people.

First, thank you to President Vincent Price for his leadership and the creation of the strategic task force on Duke's Centennial Celebration. Led by Trustee Lisa Borders, the task force provided a thoughtful vision for the Centennial that gave rise to this book.

Thank you to Jill Boy for her superb leadership and enthusiasm as executive director of Duke's Centennial Celebration and for entrusting me with this project. My never-ending gratitude goes to my partner in this endeavor, designer extraordinaire Lacey Chylack, whose boundless creativity and patience made the work a joy.

A number of Duke colleagues from across the university contributed to this book, and I am deeply grateful for their expertise and collaboration. Amy Ruth Buchanan and Jessica Ryan at Duke University Press provided project management and editorial review with consummate professional skill. Colleagues at the David M. Rubenstein Rare Book & Manuscript Library, especially Valerie Gillispie and Ani Karagianis, and at the Duke University Medical Center Library & Archives, especially Russell Koonts, Lucy Waldrop, and Rebecca Williams, offered a wealth of knowledge and assistance. Thank you to Garrett McKinnon, who conducted diligent archival research. Special thanks to Roger Lewis for his expert guidance on all things related to publishing and printing. My deep appreciation goes to Geoffrey Mock, Blyth Morrell, Gregory Phillips, and Bill Snead in University Communications & Marketing for hunting down photos and stories—and especially for our lively conversations about Duke history. Early drafts of this book were generously read by Laura Brinn, Maggie Epps, Thavolia Glymph, Dave Kennedy, Paula McClain, Deondra Rose, and Frank Tramble; their careful review and thoughtful suggestions made the book better in countless ways. Thank you also to Mike Schoenfeld for his wise advice and counsel.

Finally, my thanks go out to all the Duke faculty, staff, students, administrators, trustees, and alumni whose stories made this book possible. And to my family and friends, especially from the Class of 1990 and my graduate school days: It would take me another one hundred years to express my gratitude for your friendship and encouragement and our shared Duke memories.

This book is dedicated to all who have loved Duke University in its first one hundred years.

Carolyn Gerber '90

1920s

Trinity College's move to Durham

"Duke's History Reaches Far Afield." Working@Duke, Duke Today website, September 11, 2019, accessed at https://today.duke.edu/2019/09/dukes-history-reaches-far-afield.

James B. Duke and The Duke Endowment

Duke, James B. "Indenture and Deed of Trust Establishing The Duke Endowment." December 11, 1924, accessed at https://www.dukeendowment.org/uploads/resource-library/Duke-Indenture-times-new-roman-2022OCT21.pdf.

Durden, Robert F. *Lasting Legacy to the Carolinas: The Duke Endowment, 1924–1994.* Durham: Duke University Press, 1998.

William Preston Few

Letter to James B. Duke. Quoted in Durden, *Lasting Legacy to the Carolinas*, 7.

Remarks at the memorial service for Benjamin N. Duke. In *The Papers and Addresses of William Preston Few*, edited by Robert H. Woody, 321–22. Durham: Duke University Press, 1951, accessed at https://archive.org/details/papersaddresseso01feww/page/320/mode/2up?view=theater.

Founding of the School of Medicine

WBTW radio address by Wilburt Davison, April 9, 1929. Medical Center Archives, available at https://medspace.mc.duke.edu/concern/documents/4q77fr32b?locale=en.

"What Does Your Doctor Know? Exploring the History of Physician Education from Early Greek Theory to the Practice of Duke Medicine." Duke Libraries exhibit, 2012, accessed at https://exhibits.library.duke.edu/exhibits/show/physicianeducation/dukebeginnings.

Design and construction of West Campus

"Duke Stone: From Quarry to Campus." Working@Duke, Duke Today website, June 18, 2018, accessed at https://today.duke.edu/2018/06/duke-stone-quarry-campus.

Waring, Caroline. "Stonemasons: Carvers, Cutters, Setters." Stone by Stone website, June 26, 2018, accessed at https://stonebystone.wixsite.com/duke/post/stonemasons-carvers-cutters-setters.

Julian Abele

"Duke Names Quad in Honor of Julian Abele." Duke Today website, March 1, 2016, accessed at https://today.duke.edu/2016/03/abele.

"Julian Abele: Honoring a Legacy No Longer in 'the Shadows.'" AIA website, February 9, 2021, accessed at https://aiaeb.org/julian-abele-honoring-a-legacy-no-longer-in-the-shadows/.

"Quad Dedication Brings Julian Abele 'Out of the Shadows.'" Duke Today website, October 3, 2016, accessed at https://today.duke.edu/2016/10/quad-dedication-brings-julian-abele-out-shadows.

The Blue Devil

"The Story of the Blue Devil." GoDuke.com website, accessed at https://goduke.com/sports/2006/2/21/story_of_blue_devil.aspx.

1930s

Duke in the 1930s

Information and quote from the *Chronicle* about the opening of the School of Nursing is taken from "Looking Back at 1931: When Duke's Ambitions Took Shape." Working@Duke, Duke Today website, December 13, 2021, accessed at https://today.duke.edu/2021/12/looking-back-1931-when-duke%E2%80%99s-ambitions-took-shape.

President Few's quote is taken from "President Few Speaks at Exercises Formally Opening the New Plant." *Chronicle*, October 1, 1930, accessed at https://repository.duke.edu/dc/dukechronicle/dchnp52001.

Medical student life

"New Exhibit Features Med Student Life in 1930." Duke University Medical Center Archives website, March 2020, blog post by Caroline Waller, intern and exhibit curator, referencing the Archives exhibit "A Medical Student's Life at Duke in 1930," accessed at https://mcarchives.duke.edu/blog/new-exhibit-features-med-student-life-1930.

Duke University Marine Lab

"Mission & History." Nicholas School of the Environment website, accessed at https://nicholas.duke.edu/marinelab/about/mission-history.

College of Engineering

"Our History." Pratt School of Engineering website, accessed at https://pratt.duke.edu/about/history/.

Opening of the School of Medicine

"Medical School Opens for Work." *Chronicle*, October 1, 1930, accessed at https://repository.duke.edu/dc/dukechronicle/dchnp52001.

Scholars who came to Duke from Germany in the 1930s

"Hertha Sponer." Duke Department of Physics website, accessed at https://physics.duke.edu/about/history/historical-faculty/HerthaSponer.

King, William E. "Refugee Scholars at Duke University." In *They Fled Hitler's Germany and Found Refuge in North Carolina*, by Henry A. Landsberger and Christoph E. Schweitzer. Chapel Hill, NC: Academic Affairs Library, 1996, accessed at the Duke Department of Physics website at: https://physics.duke.edu/sites/physics.duke.edu/files/documents/RefugeeScholarsAtDukeUniversity.pdf.

William Preston Few's speech to the Class of 1931

Quoted by President Nannerl O. Keohane, Inaugural Address, October 23, 1993, accessed at https://dukespace.lib.duke.edu/dspace/bitstream/handle/10161/63/NOK19931023.pdf?sequence=1.

Opening of West Campus

"President Few Speaks at Exercises Formally Opening the New Plant." *Chronicle*, October 1, 1930, accessed at https://repository.duke.edu/dc/dukechronicle/dchnp52001.

Duke Gardens

"Dr. Hanes and the Beginnings of Duke Gardens." Duke University Medical Center Archives website, accessed at https://mcarchives.duke.edu/dr-hanes-and-beginnings-duke-gardens.

Hong, Lauren Smith. "The Women of Duke Gardens." Duke Gardens newsletter, March 2018, accessed at https://gardens.duke.edu/garden-talk-031623.

"Sarah P. Duke Gardens: How It All Began." Duke Gardens website, accessed at https://gardens.duke.edu/about/history.

Faculty houses on Campus Drive

"Built in the Early 1930s, Houses along Campus Drive Hold History." Working@Duke, Duke Today website, September 6, 2022, accessed at https://today.duke.edu/2022/09/built-early-1930s-houses-along-campus-drive-hold-history.

"List of Faculty Houses on Campus Drive." Duke University Archives website, accessed at https://library.duke.edu/rubenstein/uarchives/history/exhibits/faculty-houses-list.

Duke Chapel

Information about Duke Chapel and quote from James B. Duke are from the Duke Chapel website, accessed at https://chapel.duke.edu/about-chapel.

Duke Forest

Information about Duke Forest is from the Duke Forest website, including the following pages:

"About Duke Forest," accessed at https://dukeforest.duke.edu/about/.

"The Duke Forest Log." Bulletin from the Office of the Duke Forest, Fall 2020, accessed at https://dukeforest.duke.edu/files/2020/12/2020LOG_digital.pdf.

"11 Interesting Facts about the Duke Forest," accessed at https://dukeforest.spotlight.duke.edu/.

"History," accessed at https://dukeforest.duke.edu/home/history/.

Richard H. Brodhead

Quoted in "A Shared Fate between Academics, Athletics, Medicine and Location." Faculty Address, Duke University, March 19, 2015, accessed at https://today.duke.edu/2015/03/rhbaddress.

Studying the Paranormal at Duke

"The Letter Compels You!" Bitstreams, Duke University Libraries, October 31, 2017, blog post by Alex Marsh, accessed at https://blogs.library.duke.edu/bitstreams/2017/10/31/the-letter-compels-you/.

1940s

This chapter acknowledges with gratitude two online exhibits: "From Campus to Cockpit: Duke during WWII." Duke University Libraries, accessed at https://exhibits.library.duke.edu/exhibits/show/fromcampustocockpit/intro.

"Remembering the 65th: Duke's General Hospital Unit." Duke Medical Center Archives, accessed at https://exhibits.mclibrary.duke.edu/sixty-fifth/introduction.html.

Robert Frost

"A Mood Apart." First edition broadside poem (1945), published in conjunction with Frost's visit to Duke University Libraries, accessed at https://www.qbbooks.com/pages/books/49100/robert-frost/a-mood-apart-a-rare-broadside-keepsake.

William Styron

West, James L. W., III. "William Styron at Duke, 1943–44." *Southern Literary Journal* 28, no. 1 (Fall 1995): 5–18, accessed at https://www.jstor.org/stable/20078134.

Raphael Lemkin

Information about the Lemkin Rule of Law Guardians is from the program website, accessed at https://judicialstudies.duke.edu/programs/lemkin-rule-of-law-guardians/.

"The Secret Game"
Ellsworth, Scott. "Jim Crow Loses; The Secret Game." *New York Times Magazine*, March 31, 1996, accessed at https://nccueaglepride.com/sports/2011/3/8/MBB_0308110905.aspx.
Ellsworth, Scott. "The Secret Game: Defying the Color Line." *Duke Magazine*, March 2010, accessed at https://nccueaglepride.com/documents/2011/3/8/DukeUAlumniMagazineSecretGame.pdf?id=162.
Ellsworth, Scott. *The Secret Game: A Wartime Story of Courage, Change, and Basketball's Lost Triumph.* Boston: Little, Brown, 2016.

George Wall and George-Frank Wall
Glymph, Thavolia. Unpublished research, 2023.
McDonald, Thomasi. "East Campus Union Renamed for Longtime Custodians." Duke Today website, February 27, 2024, accessed at https://today.duke.edu/2024/02/east-campus-union-renamed-longtime-custodians.
"One Hundred Reasons." *Duke Magazine*, Fall 2012, accessed at https://alumni.duke.edu/magazine/articles/one-hundred-reasons.
Van Brocklin, Elizabeth. "The Legacy of Duke's First Janitor." *Duke Magazine*, Spring 2015, accessed at https://alumni.duke.edu/magazine/articles/legacy-dukes-first-janitor.

Juanita Kreps
"Notable Alumna: Juanita Kreps." One of a series of profiles on notable Duke Graduate School alumni. The Graduate School website, March 3, 2016, accessed at https://gradschool.duke.edu/story/notable-alumna-juanita-kreps/.

1950s

1951 Duke-Temple basketball game
Featherston, Al. "1951 Duke-Temple Game Broke Color Barriers." GoDuke.com website, February 23, 2011, accessed at https://goduke.com/news/2011/2/23/205102054.aspx.

Duke's medical curriculum
"Engaging Students in Dedicated Research and Scholarship during Medical School: The Long-Term Experiences at Duke and Stanford." *Academic Medicine* 85, no. 3 (March, 2010): 419–28, accessed at https://pubmed.ncbi.nlm.nih.gov/20182114/.

Hollis Edens
Woody, Robert H. "Edens, Arthur Hollis." NCPedia, 1986, accessed at https://www.ncpedia.org/biography/edens-arthur-hollis.

Duke Center for the Study of Aging and Human Development
Duke Center for the Study of Aging and Human Development website, accessed at https://agingcenter.duke.edu/history.
George, Linda K., Erdman Palmore, and Harvey J. Cohen. "The Duke Center for the Study of Aging: One of Our Earliest Roots." *Gerontologist* 54, no. 1 (2014): 59–66, accessed at https://pubmed.ncbi.nlm.nih.gov/23733867/.
Maddox, George L. Ten-part history of the Aging Center from the *Center Report*, accessed at https://agingcenter.duke.edu/sites/default/files/2022-04/center-history-complete-series.pdf.

Marcus Hobbs
"Former Provost Marcus Hobbs Dies." Duke Today website, August 17, 2007, accessed at https://today.duke.edu/2007/08/hobbs.html.

Research Triangle Park (RTP)
Abbott, Morgan P. "North Carolina's Research Triangle Park: A Success Story of Private Industry Fostering Public Investment to Create a Homegrown Commercial Park." *Campbell Law Review* 40, no. 569 (2018), accessed at https://scholarship.law.campbell.edu/cgi/viewcontent.cgi?article=1659&context=clr.
RTP website, accessed at https://www.rtp.org/history/.

Sally Dalton Robinson
"Alumni Love Affair with Duke." *Duke Magazine*, October 1, 2006, accessed at https://alumni.duke.edu/magazine/articles/alumni-love-affair-duke.

Quote by Sally Dalton Robinson: Episode 85, "Sally Robinson: People and Possibility." Interview on the "On Life and Meaning" podcast, February 22, 2019, accessed at https://www.youtube.com/watch?v=fc9LQeUQQTY.

Women at Duke in the 1950s
Handbooks published by the Social Standards Committee, part of the Woman's Student Government Association (1930–1972), accessed at https://repository.duke.edu/dc/uawomanshandbook.
"It's Not in the Handbook, 1950–1951," accessed at https://dukelibraries.contentdm.oclc.org/digital/collection/p15957coll25/id/283/.

Jewish Life at Duke in the 1950s
Waldman, Charlene Nachman. "Jewish Life at Duke in the 1950s." Duke Student Affairs website, accessed at https://students.duke.edu/jewish-life-at-duke-in-the-1950s/.

Dave Sime
Roth, John. "Appreciating Duke Legend Dave Sime." *GoDuke: The Magazine*, March 7, 2016, accessed at https://goduke.com/news/2016/3/7/210765725.aspx.

1960s

The Gross-Edens Affair
Durden, Robert F. "Donnybrook at Duke: The Gross-Edens Affair of 1960: Parts I & II." *North Carolina Historical Review* 71, no. 4 (October 1994): 451–71, accessed at https://www.jstor.org/stable/23521823?seq=21.
Knight, Douglas M. *Street of Dreams: The Nature and Legacy of the 1960s.* Durham: Duke University Press, 1989.

Krueger Report
Final Report of the Ad Hoc Duke Interdisciplinary Priorities Committee: Overarching Analysis and Recommendations for Academic Council, May 2021, accessed at https://sites.duke.edu/interdisciplinary/files/2021/06/interdisciplinary-priorities-committee-report-duke-ac.pdf.

The Allen Building takeover
Segal, Theodore D. *Point of Reckoning: The Fight for Racial Justice at Duke University*. Durham: Duke University Press, 2021.

The first five Black undergraduates at Duke
"Legacy, 1963–1993: Thirty Years of African-American Students at Duke University." Duke University, Office of the University Vice President and Vice Provost, 1995, accessed at https://ia800607.us.archive.org/18/items/legacy19631993th00duke/legacy19631993th00duke.pdf.

Wilhelmina Reuben-Cooke
Quoted in Bridget Booher, "The First Five Undergraduates," *Duke Magazine*, September–October 1992, reprinted in "Legacy, 1963–1993: Thirty Years of African-American Students at Duke University."

Brenda Armstrong
Knight, Douglas M. *The Dancer and the Dance*. New York: Separate Star, 2003.
Quoted in Bridget Booher, "Let's Talk about Race," *Duke Magazine*, Spring 2013, accessed at https://alumni.duke.edu/magazine/articles/lets-talk-about-race.

1970s
Duke Cancer Institute
"Duke Celebrates 50 Years of Cancer Care—and Looks toward the Next 50." Duke Cancer Institute, July 7, 2022, accessed at https://cancerhistoryproject.com/institutions/duke-celebrates-50-years-of-cancer-care-and-looks-toward-the-next-50/.

President Terry Sanford
"This Kind of University." Excerpt from inaugural address, October 18, 1970, Duke University Archives, accessed at https://dukespace.lib.duke.edu/items/13ab7453-fa6b-4586-bf37-f0b06dd306cd.

Professor Mark Anthony Neal
Quoted in "Always in Motion: 50 Years of Black Studies at Duke," January 21, 2020, compiled and edited by Camille Jackson, Kathryn Kennedy, and Matt Hartman, accessed at https://trinity.duke.edu/news/always-motion-50-years-black-studies-duke.

Raymond Gavins
"Duke Flags Lowered; Pioneering Historian Raymond Gavins Dies." Duke Today website, May 23, 2016, accessed at https://today.duke.edu/2016/05/gavinsobit.

Public Policy at Duke
"Celebrating 50 Years of Public Policy at Duke University." Sanford School website, October 7, 2021, accessed at https://sanford.duke.edu/story/celebrating-50-years-public-policy-duke-university/.
"Creating Public Policy at Duke," accessed at https://static.sanford.duke.edu/50years/impact/index.html.

Women's Athletics at Duke
"Duke Announces 50 Years of Women's Varsity Athletics Celebration." GoDuke.com website, July 14, 2021, accessed at https://goduke.com/news/2021/7/14/duke-announces-50-years-of-womens-varsity-athletics-celebration.aspx.

Al Buehler
"Duke Athletics Hall of Fame Member Al Buehler Passes Away." GoDuke.com website, January 10, 2023, accessed at https://goduke.com/news/2023/1/10/track-field-duke-athletics-hall-of-fame-member-al-buehler-passes-away.aspx.
"Trail Name Honors Longtime Track Coach." Duke Today website, September 15, 2000, accessed at https://today.duke.edu/2000/09/buehler915.html.

1980s
Mike Krzyzewski
"1980: Coach K Introduced at Duke." WRALSportsFan website, accessed at https://www.wralsportsfan.com/duke/video/14738424/.

President H. Keith H. Brodie
Essay published in the *Chanticleer* 1987 yearbook, p. 90.

Duke Human Vaccine Institute
"History." Duke Human Vaccine Institute website, accessed at https://dhvi.duke.edu/about-us/history.
Schramm, Stephen. "On the Early Front Lines in the HIV/AIDS Fight." Working@Duke, Duke Today website, November 30, 2022, accessed at https://today.duke.edu/2022/11/early-front-lines-hivaids-fight.

President Terry Sanford
Gillispie, Valerie. "Uncle Terry Saves the Day." *Duke Magazine*, Fall 2017, accessed at https://alumni.duke.edu/magazine/articles/uncle-terry-saves-day.
"Uncle Terry." Letter in University Archives, accessed at https://www.flickr.com/photos/dukeyearlook/12039383323.

1990s
Duke in the 1990s
"Building Community of Interest: Report of the Task Force on the Intellectual Climate at Duke University." Duke University, April 1994, accessed at https://dukespace.lib.duke.edu/dspace/bitstream/handle/10161/3190/Task%20Force%20on%20Intellectual%20Climate%201994.pdf?sequence=1&isAllowed=y.
Price, Reynolds. Founders' Day address, 1992, University Archives.
Willimon, William H. "Old Duke—New Duke: A Report to the President." Duke University, November 2000, accessed at https://collegiateway.org/pdf/willimon-2000.pdf.
Willimon, William H. "We Work Hard, We Play Hard: A Report for the President and the Provost, and the Vice President for Student Life of Duke University." Duke University, April 25, 1993, accessed at https://dukespace.lib.duke.edu/dspace/bitstream/handle/10161/77/WorkHard.pdf?sequence=1.

President Nannerl O. Keohane
Keohane, Nannerl O. Inaugural Address, October 23, 1993, accessed at https://dukespace.lib.duke.edu/dspace/bitstream/handle/10161/63/NOK19931023.pdf?sequence=1.

"Nannerl O. Keohane: Her Presidency Has Changed Duke's Sense of the Possible." University Medal citation. Duke Today website, October 2, 2003, accessed at https://today.duke.edu/2003/10/keohanemedalo03.html.

"The Transforming Experience of Being around a University." Founders' Day Address, October 2, 2003, Duke Today website, accessed at https://today.duke.edu/2003/10/founderskeohaneo03.html.

Undergraduate admissions

Dagger, Jacob. "Top of the Crop." *Duke Magazine*, January–February 2006, accessed at https://alumni.duke.edu/magazine/articles/top-crop.

Black Faculty Initiative

Mock, Geoffrey. "Finding Duke's Front Door." Part of the Diversity and Excellence Series, Duke Today website, December 2, 2009, accessed at https://today.duke.edu/2009/12/bfimain.html.

Advancing Health

"History." Duke Health website, accessed at https://corporate.dukehealth.org/who-we-are/history.

2000s

Duke Women's Initiative

"A Happy Reunion for the Woman's College." Duke Today website, November 13, 2002, accessed at https://today.duke.edu/2002/11/reunion1102.html.

"Nannerl O. Keohane: Women's Contributions to Duke." Duke Today website, November 12, 2002, accessed at https://today.duke.edu/2002/11/womans-college1102.html.

"Nannerl O. Keohane: The Women's Initiative." Duke Today website, November 12, 2002, accessed at https://today.duke.edu/2002/10/2womcoll1102.html.

Women's Initiative Steering Committee. *Women's Initiative Report*. Duke University Libraries, 2003, accessed at https://hdl.handle.net/10161/8410.

President Richard H. Brodhead

Brodhead, Richard, H. *Speaking of Duke: Leading the Twenty-First-Century University*. Durham: Duke University Press, 2017.

"Constructing Duke." Convocation Address, August 19, 2015, accessed at https://today.duke.edu/2015/08/rhbconvoc15.

"More Day to Dawn." Inaugural Address, September 18, 2004, accessed at https://hdl.handle.net/10161/2656.

Speaking about DukeEngage. DukeEngage website, accessed at https://dukeengage.duke.edu/brodhead/.

Interdisciplinary studies at Duke

Balleisen, Edward. "The Evolution of Interdisciplinarity at Duke: A Brief Historical Excursion through the Lens of Strategic Planning." *Report for Academic Council*, May 2021, accessed at https://sites.duke.edu/interdisciplinary/files/2021/06/evolution-interdisciplinarity-duke-ac.pdf.

John Hope Franklin

"Biography of Dr. John Hope Franklin." John Hope Franklin Center website, accessed at https://jhfc.duke.edu/jhfbio/.

"A Franklin Celebration." Duke Today website, June 11, 2009, accessed at https://today.duke.edu/2009/06/franklinfolo.html.

"John Hope Franklin, Scholar Who Transformed African-American History, Dies at 94." Duke Today website, March 25, 2009, accessed at https://today.duke.edu/2009/03/johnhopefranklin.html.

Raymond D. Nasher

"Raymond D. Nasher: Namesake and Founder." Nasher Museum of Art website, November 8, 2015, accessed at https://nasher.duke.edu/stories/raymond-d-nasher-namesake-and-founder/.

2010s

President Richard H. Brodhead

Bliwise, Robert J. "A Look at the Brodhead Legacy." *Duke Magazine*, Winter 2016, accessed at https://alumni.duke.edu/magazine/articles/look-brodhead-legacy.

"The Heart of the Matter: The Humanities and Social Sciences for a Vibrant, Competitive, and Secure Nation." *Report by the Commission on the Humanities and Social Sciences*, American Academy of Arts and Sciences, 2013, accessed at https://www.amacad.org/publication/heart-matter.

"President Brodhead Brings the Humanities to 'The Colbert Report,'" Duke Today website, August 16, 2013, accessed at https://today.duke.edu/2013/08/colbertrhb.

"President Richard Brodhead to Step Down in 2017." Duke Today website, April 28, 2016, accessed at https://today.duke.edu/2016/04/brodheadannouncement.

Mary Duke Biddle Trent Semans

Brodhead, Richard H. *Speaking of Duke: Leading the Twenty-First-Century University*. Durham: Duke University Press, 2017, 127.

"Mary Semans, Champion of Duke and Durham, Dies." Duke Today website, January 25, 2012, accessed at https://today.duke.edu/2012/01/marysemans.

Bass Connections

Information for Bass Connections taken from the Bass Connections website, accessed at https://bassconnections.duke.edu/.

Robert J. Lefkowitz and Paul Modrich

"A Look at Duke's Nobel Laureates." Duke Today website, October 5, 2020, accessed at https://today.duke.edu/2020/10/look-dukes-nobel-laureates.

Duke Forward campaign

"Duke Campaign Raises $3.85 Billion to Empower Service to Society." Duke Today website, August 9, 2017, accessed at https://today.duke.edu/2017/08/duke-campaign-raises-385-billion-empower-service-society.

"Moving Duke and the World Forward." Duke University, 2017, accessed at https://impact.dukeforward.duke.edu/.

President Vincent E. Price

"Price Address Connects Duke's Historic Strengths to New Initiatives." Duke Today website, March 23, 2018, accessed at https://today.duke.edu/2018/03/price-address-connects-dukes-historic-strengths-new-initiatives.

"Vincent E. Price: 'Again We Are Called Upon to Answer the Challenges of the Day.'" Inaugural Address, October 5, 2017, Duke Today website, accessed at https://today.duke.edu/2017/10/vincent-e-price-again-we-are-called-upon-answer-challenges-day.

Rev. Dr. Luke A. Powery

Quoted in "President's Message on Duke Chapel Space." Duke Today website, August 16, 2018, accessed at https://today.duke.edu/2018/08/presidents-message-duke-chapel-space.

Dedication of Abele Quad

"Quad Dedication Brings Julian Abele 'Out of the Shadows.'" Duke Today website, October 3, 2016, accessed at https://today.duke.edu/2016/10/quad-dedication-brings-julian-abele-out-shadows.

2013 Commemoration of the fiftieth anniversary of the enrollment of the first Black undergraduates

"Celebrating the Past, Charting the Future: Commemorating 50 Years of Black Students at Duke." Duke University website, accessed at https://spotlight.duke.edu/50years/.

2020s

President Vincent E. Price

"Statement from President Price on Juneteenth Celebration and Next Steps on Addressing Racism." Duke Today website, June 17, 2020, accessed at https://today.duke.edu/2020/06/statement-president-price-juneteenth-celebration-and-next-steps-addressing-racism.

"Strategic Vision." Duke University, accessed at https://strategicvision.duke.edu/.

"Urgent Message Regarding COVID-19." Duke University, March 10, 2020, accessed at https://president.duke.edu/2020/03/10/urgent-message-regarding-covid-19/.

A. Eugene Washington

"Chancellor Washington Provides His Thoughts about Recent Tragedies." Duke Health website, June 1, 2020, accessed at https://corporate.dukehealth.org/events/chancellor-washington-provides-his-thoughts-about-recent-tragedies.

Athletics

"Duke's Mike Krzyzewski: 'Black Lives Matter' a Human Rights Statement, Not a Political One." ESPN, June 26, 2020, accessed at https://www.espn.com/mens-college-basketball/story/_/id/29371614/black-lives-matter-human-rights-statement-not-political-one.

"Men's Basketball Spearheads Peaceful Protest." GoDuke.com website, August 27, 2020, accessed at https://goduke.com/news/2020/8/27/mens-basketball-spearheads-campus-rally.aspx.

Duke's response to the COVID-19 pandemic

Denny, T. N., L. Andrews, and M. Bonsignori, et al. "Implementation of a Pooled Surveillance Testing Program for Asymptomatic SARS-CoV-2 Infections on a College Campus—Duke University, Durham, North Carolina, August 2–October 11, 2020." *Morbidity and Mortality Weekly Report* 69 (2020): 1743–47, accessed at https://www.cdc.gov/mmwr/volumes/69/wr/mm6946e1.htm.

"Duke University's Aggressive COVID Testing and Surveillance Minimized Infections." Duke Health website, November 17, 2020, accessed at https://corporate.dukehealth.org/news/duke-universitys-aggressive-covid-testing-and-surveillance-minimized-infections.

Faye Williams, quoted in "An Amazing Day." Duke Today website, December 15, 2020, accessed at https://today.duke.edu/2020/12/amazing-day.

Mary E. Klotman, quoted in "A Video of Thanks Highlighting the School of Medicine's Response to COVID-19." Duke Today website, April 4, 2021, accessed at https://today.duke.edu/2021/04/video-thanks-highlighting-school-medicines-response-covid-19.

Miller, Ben. "Duke Faculty Fight for Latinx Communities Hit Hard by COVID-19." Duke School of Medicine, *Magnify* magazine, January 26, 2021, accessed at https://medschool.duke.edu/stories/duke-faculty-fight-latinx-communities-hit-hard-covid-19.

Schramm, Stephen. "Nearly 1 Million Tests Mark End to Part of Duke's COVID-19 Response." Working@Duke, Duke Today website, March 22, 2023, accessed at https://today.duke.edu/2023/03/nearly-1-million-tests-mark-end-part-dukes-covid-19-response.

Duke and Durham

Strategic Community Impact Plan. Duke's Office of Durham and Community Affairs, accessed at https://community.duke.edu/priorities/.

Kate Bowler

Mock, Geoffrey. "A Durham Mural Becomes a Destination for the Heart-Sore." Duke Today website, October 14, 2022, accessed at https://today.duke.edu/2022/10/durham-mural-becomes-destination-heart-sore.

Research Translation and Commercialization

Schramm, Stephen. "Duke Spotlight: Office for Translation and Commercialization Turns Smart Ideas into Reality." Working@Duke, Duke Today website, August 15, 2023, accessed at https://today.duke.edu/2023/08/duke-spotlight-office-translation-commercialization-turns-smart-ideas-reality.

PHOTO CREDITS
with APPRECIATION

UNLESS OTHERWISE NOTED, all images appearing in this book were sourced from the Duke University Archives in the David M. Rubenstein Rare Book & Manuscript Library, Duke University Medical Center Archives, Duke University Communications & Marketing, *Duke Magazine*, Duke Athletics, DukeEngage, the Rubenstein Arts Center, the Nasher Museum of Art, Sarah P. Duke Gardens, the Duke Lemur Center, the Duke Campus Farm, the Duke University Marine Lab, Duke Kunshan University, Duke-NUS Medical School in Singapore, and the *Chanticleer*, Duke University's annual student yearbook.

SPECIAL THANKS also to the *Chronicle*, Duke University's independent student news organization, for sharing images for inclusion in this book.

Sourced from **WIKIPEDIA:**
Page 44: Juanita M. Kreps, Ph.D.
Page 63: J. Deryl Hart House by Willthacheerleader18; https://en.wikipedia.org/wiki/J._Deryl_Hart_House
Page 68: Matthew A. Zimmerman
Page 127: Nobel Prize medals

OTHER Sources:
Page 124: Portrait of Raymond D. Nasher taken from "Dallas Businessman to Build, Donate $32 Million Sculpture Garden Downtown." *Dallas Chamber Report* 35, no. 5 (May 1997).
Page 143: Whale research image by Kevin Bierlich Ph.D.'21 as part of the Duke Marine Robotics and Remote Sensing Lab.